SERIES ON
ECONOMIC DEVELOPMENT
AND GROWTH VOL. 5

NARRATIVES OF
CHINESE ECONOMIC REFORMS:
HOW DOES CHINA CROSS
THE RIVER?

Series on Economic Development and Growth   (ISSN: 1793-3668)

SERIES ON
ECONOMIC DEVELOPMENT
AND GROWTH   VOL. 5

NARRATIVES OF CHINESE ECONOMIC REFORMS: HOW DOES CHINA CROSS THE RIVER?

Edited by

Xiaobo Zhang
Shenggen Fan
International Food Policy Research Institute, USA

Arjan de Haan
Institute of Social Studies, The Netherlands

 **World Scientific**

NEW JERSEY · LONDON · SINGAPORE · BEIJING · SHANGHAI · HONG KONG · TAIPEI · CHENNAI

Published by

World Scientific Publishing Co. Pte. Ltd.

5 Toh Tuck Link, Singapore 596224

USA office: 27 Warren Street, Suite 401-402, Hackensack, NJ 07601

UK office: 57 Shelton Street, Covent Garden, London WC2H 9HE

British Library Cataloguing-in-Publication Data
A catalogue record for this book is available from the British Library.

Series on Economic Development and Growth — Vol. 5
NARRATIVES OF CHINESE ECONOMIC REFORMS
How Does China Cross the River?

ISBN-13 978-981-4293-30-3
ISBN-10 981-4293-30-X

Typeset by Stallion Press
Email: enquiries@stallionpress.com

Printed in Singapore.

PREFACE

Rapid growth in the Chinese economy in the past three decades poses puzzles and challenges to neo-classical economic theory, as policies implemented during the reform process were often unorthodox. Although the Chinese experience has been widely studied, myths and questions about the reforms remain.

To fill the knowledge gap, and to inform a process of learning from China's development successes, IFPRI and DFID commissioned a series of case studies on the policy process of different initiatives, including rural transformation, dual-track price reform, village election, migration policy, and rural industrialization. Five of these papers were prepared for and discussed during the Global Development Network conference in Beijing, January 12–19, 2007; others were prepared and commissioned subsequently, for example in the context of the celebration of China's 30 years of reform in 2008.

This intellectual project was inspired by the essay on China's rural reform by Mr. Du Runsheng, the father of China's rural reform (published by IFPRI in 2006). The present collection of papers extends the analysis of initial rural reforms on which Mr. Du focused. Subsequent reforms emphasized broader issues such as markets and prices, rural/urban migration, taxation, and local governance. These later reforms fundamentally began the transformation of China from a largely agrarian and poor country to a middle-income and industrial country, although China remains at an early stage of industrialization with rampant poverty, particularly in western and central regions.

Uniquely, many of the authors of the case studies were deeply involved in these reforms, either through direct policymaking or through providing analytical and technical support that have led to these policy changes. They provide a first-hand account of the policy processes and demonstrate from their experience ways to promote policy reforms.

With in-depth insight, they highlight *how* the political processes took place, how social and political entrepreneurs shaped the choices and sequences of various reforms, and overcame the rigidities and sometimes erroneous beliefs. This is essential because policy processes are often a *de facto* "black box" to which erroneous beliefs about the policy process are often prescribed as reality.

The narratives by these authors provide important insights for other developing countries in their attempts to design their reform and development agendas. As China is increasingly held up as a model for development, we believe, it is crucial to ensure that its lessons are told, in all its complexities. This volume makes a modest contribution to articulating these lessons.

ACKNOWLEDGMENTS

Thanks are due to all the chapter authors. We have received excellent administrative support from Rowena L. Natividad and research support from Lisa Moorman from IFPRI, which we acknowledge with appreciation. We are also grateful for the translation of several chapters from Chinese into English by David Kelly. Funding support from the Department for International Development in the UK is gratefully acknowledged.

Xiaobo Zhang
Arjan de Haan
Shenggen Fan

CONTENTS

CHAPTER 1

INTRODUCTION: POLICY REFORMS AS A PROCESS OF LEARNING

Xiaobo Zhang, Arjan de Haan and Shenggen Fan

The rapid growth in the Chinese economy despite the fact that its economic institutions and policies appear gravely inadequate against the propositions of mainstream economic theory has posed many puzzles to development economists. As pointed out by Summers (2007), in the past three decades, China has experienced the same degree of industrialization that took two centuries to occur in Europe. While many foreign observers frequently highlight the institutional constraints hindering China's development progress, it continues to have maintained record levels of economic growth and poverty reduction. The Chinese experience has been widely studied (Qian, 2003; Fan, Zhang, and Zhang, 2004; Hofman and Wu, 2007; Lin, 2007; Ravallion, 2007). For example, Lin (2007) argues that China's rapid growth is due to its shift in development strategy from capital intensive to labor intensive, in line with China's comparative advantage. However, there are still many myths and questions about the internal processes and logic that drove the reform. Most of the previous studies provide *ex post* assessment of the major reform measures, yet offer little insight into the internal, political processes of reform.

Many of the approaches used in the reform process are unorthodox from a standard neo-classical paradigm (Rodrik, 2004). It is possible that heterodox reform measures may be too China-specific to be transferable to other countries, but some of the policies and strategies behind the reform process may transcend international borders, and we believe in the potential of drawing out the lessons from China's development path for the broader development community. The successes of these reforms may challenge traditional neo-classical economic theory, and the much debated Washington or post-Washington Consensus.

We follow a framework on the process of economic change developed by North (2005). He views development as arising from incremental steps by many decentralized agents which shape the formal rules and informal norms and hence the overall economies. Policy change entails uncertainty to human beings. People often have different interpretations of the uncertainty associated with proposed change, and each interest group has its own perceived payoffs and risks from proposed policy changes. In essence, reforms are ways to break the existing, less desirable equilibrium among different interest groups and move it to a more favorable one. Facing a binding constraint, there are potentially many solutions. Therefore, successful reform strategies help to enlarge the choice sets, reduce the perceived risks, and improve the understanding of potential payoffs of different policy options.

To understand how the reform process in China originated and why it succeeded, distinguished policymakers and researchers who were involved in the reform process present their textured and first-hand accounts of the reform process. This narrative approach provides a rich story about the reform processes and is instrumental in helping generate hypotheses which can be tested by quantitative methods. Several common themes emerge from the case studies. The key ingredients are summarized here, focusing on the use of crisis as an opportunity, experimentation with regionally-specific policy formulation and reform, sequencing, information flow and consultation, and institutional capacity in addressing barriers to reforms.

1.1. Use the Crisis as an Opportunity

Vested interest groups evaluate the risks and payoffs with regard to the consequence of proposed policy change. People often have different perceptions of the uncertainty related to change. Although crisis is bad by definition, it may help radically revise perceived risks and payoffs of certain policy options. A crisis can also redesign policy priorities where new approaches emerge out of previous failures, a process that we are witnessing during 2008–2009 after the financial crisis, with a radical reorientation towards a more inward-oriented development model, and intense political discussion about the directions of these reforms. Despite the negative effects of any crisis, crises necessitate change and re-examinations of current policies. We use several examples in this book to illustrate how crisis may beget reform.

After the Cultural Revolution (1966–1976), China was on the verge of collapse under the planned economy system. More than two-thirds of people lived under one dollar per day (Ravallion, 2007). With stagnant agricultural growth and fast population growth, food was in short supply. At the onset of reform, it seemed China faced extremely high barriers to escaping the low-level equilibrium trap where poverty persisted. However, as shown in the chapter by Du Runsheng, one of the architects of China's rural reform, a crisis may trigger reforms. After the end of the Cultural Revolution, both the top leaders and masses realized that the planned system was not a viable option anymore and there was a consensus to change it. Under this circumstance, the top leaders were more willing to listen to different opinions and to allow open policy debate. In other words, crises may provide reformers with a window of opportunity to push their reform agenda. Reforms do not come automatically and require policymakers to seize this as an opportunity. Reform policies must be developed in a timely fashion after crises to be a legitimate alternative.

One noted example is the rural reform documented by Du, presented in Chapter 2 of this volume. Farmers who experienced the Great Famine in the late 1950s and early 1960s still had a vivid memory of the disaster and they knew the collective farming did not work in times of crises. So with another imminent weather shock looming in 1977, the local government in Fengyang County, Anhui Province, decided to contract the collective land to farmers because they knew the collective farming system could lead to another famine in the event of a severe shock. Yao (2007) provides an extensive review of land tenure changes in rural China. He argues that when the household responsibility system (HRS) was scaled up, despite some initial resistance, most farmers welcomed the reform measure wholeheartedly because they knew collective farming did not work.

China's village elections, described in Chapter 6 by Wang Zhenyao, are another notable example. Until the mid-1980s, both the head and party secretary of a village were appointed by the upper-level government. With the rapid abolition of people's communes, and the shift of production from collective farming to the household responsibility system in the late 1970s, the appointed leaders lost their political legitimacy. Many villages failed to provide basic public goods and services. The conflict between cadres and villagers over taxation became increasingly serious. Facing this pressure, the central government started to embrace the idea of grassroots elections, previously taboo, by giving local people a larger say in their local affairs. After several years of experimentation, the central government called for widespread implementation in the early 1990s.

The third example is the Wenzhou model, described by Zhu Kangdui in Chapter 5 of this volume. Wenzhou used to be one of the poorest regions in China. At the war frontier to Taiwan in the planned economic era, the central government had made little public investment in the region. Together with geographical isolation and high population/land ratio, many people fled elsewhere to escape starvation. Because they were so poor prior to reforms, Wenzhou people wanted to change to have a better life. The local government officials respected popular demand. They lobbied the central government to grant them permission to conduct policy experiments on rural industrialization in Wenzhou. They supported the grassroots reforms of vast number of entrepreneurs to overcome institutional barriers faced by private enterprises. At the time, it was illegal for a private enterprise to hire more than eight workers. In order to avoid direct conflicts with the legal system and to reduce the high transaction costs caused by branding, many private enterprises resorted to some makeshift practices such as attaching themselves to a legal enterprise or organization to avoid the ownership risk of hiring more than eight workers in a private firm. Local governments accepted these practices as well. In addition to allowing those "wearing red hats" (private firms registered as TVEs), the local government conducted many institutional reforms to create an enabling environment for private business. Not only have Wenzhou's reforms promoted its local economy, but they have also provided valuable experience for China as a whole.

1.2. Crossing the River by Touching the Stones

Having observed the disastrous performance of the ideology-based process in the planned economy era, such as the Great Famine (1959–1961) and the Cultural Revolution (1966–1976), in 1978 the Communist Party's 11th Congress shifted the policymaking process from ideology-based to evidence-based under the slogan of "seeking truths from facts". This approach places great weight on demonstrated evidence on the ground instead of on theory. The policymakers adopted a programmatic attitude toward reform ("crossing the river by touching the stones"). The success of the economic reform in the past 30 years triumphs the virtues of this incremental reform strategy. All the chapters in this book illustrate one of the distinguishing features of China's reform experience — that economic success has been a process of gradual and sequential reforms, consciously avoiding "big-bang" approaches. Pragmatism, trial and error, and experimentation with small-scale policy reforms that are later scaled up are key features of China's reforms.

Learning by experimentation is a key strategy in reforms, particularly when facing huge uncertainty. When facing choices never seen before, it is extremely risky for agents to make radical choices. In such circumstances, experimentation can be a useful tool to search for more information and test and update hypotheses. Experiments yield information to help understand what works and what does not work. Even failures can be helpful because they can help eliminate unfavorable options, as shown by Luo Xiaopeng's case study (Chapter 3). The failure of his price reform experiment in Hebei Province helped him come up with the idea of dual-track price reform. Although this idea was dismissed by Murphy *et al.* (1992) as provoking drops in output in the Soviet Union due to increased arbitrage and corruption, the dual-track price reform is an important example of an experiment where the "Washington Consensus" wisdom was contradicted.

The multi-faceted fiscal and tax reforms described in Chapter 7 by Liu Zhongli and in Chapter 8 by Weng Lihua similarly show the gradual (and long-term) nature of successful reform. The fiscal reforms of the early reform phase contributed towards decentralization, but greatly reduced the national fiscal income. Reforms in the first half of the 1990s involved a range of measures to allocate taxes between governments and state-owned enterprises (SOEs), creation of separate state and regional tax bureaus, and ways to link tax returns to regional economic growth rates — and as Liu Zhongli emphasizes, the optimization of resource allocation in the context of Chinese specific circumstances remains a challenge.

Moreover, experimentation can help control the possible disastrous consequence of wrong choices. A wrong choice, at large scale, may be irreversible, and therefore may undermine political stability and weaken the learning capacity. Most of the experiments presented in this book were not random. Most of the experiments started in isolated, poor areas. As shown in the chapter by Du, the leaders purposely situated the pilot experiment of the household responsibility reform in remote provinces to avoid negative spillovers and to reduce political resistance. One reason that Wenzhou received the special permission to be a pilot of rural industrialization was because of its rather isolated location at the time. Overall, most experiments were insulated from the wider society and economy. This means that in the event of failure, repercussions are contained. It should be noted that these experiments were not randomly designed as advocated by mainstream development economists (Duflo, 2005).

The experiments and demonstrations allow individuals to become acquainted with proposed changes, to reduce perceived risk and to better understand the possible payoffs. As vividly documented in Wang Zhenyao's case study (Chapter 6), China conducted numerous pilots of village elections before scaling up. When the idea of village elections was first put forward, it received strong resistance. Nonetheless, the central government encouraged some provinces to conduct pilot experiments. The success of these experiments helped reduce the perceived risks of village self-governance. This led the People's Congress to pass the implementation amendments to the Organic Law in 1992.

Similar to the pilot stage, in the implementation stage too many counties followed a two-step process. First, the county civil affairs bureau selected several townships for the village elections experiment. In the second step, the county civil affairs bureau analyzed and summarized the experience from pilot experiments, adjusted election rules, and then encouraged countywide elections. Throughout the whole process, the civil affairs bureau organized many meetings to facilitate the exchange of experiences and lessons. The descriptions of fiscal reforms in Chapters 7 and 8 similarly highlight the consultative nature of reforms, and in the case of Zhejiang Province the space for regional differences in policy implementation.

The post-Mao era in China adopted an evidence-based policymaking process. Most successful reforms have undergone pilot experiments and impact evolutions before being scaled up. Although the experiments were not rigorously and scientifically conducted by including control groups, the pilots enabled researchers to observe what worked and what did not on the ground.

1.3. Right Sequencing is Crucial

One of the lessons from the Chinese reform experience is the right sequence of reform policies. Beginning with agriculture ensured that the majority of the population benefited from the initial reforms (for example, the increase in the procurement price), given the overwhelming dependence of the population on the primary sector. The large number of prospective beneficiaries also helped generate consensus and create political support for the subsequent stages of the reform process. The various incentive reforms — including the new land tenure laws, the rise in procurement prices, marketing reforms, and exchange rate interventions — led to an improvement in returns for farmers and in the efficiency of resource allocation in the economy. As a result, the domestic production base was strengthened and gradually made more competitive.

Integration into the world market through trade liberalization was attempted only *after* these land, price and other reforms were successfully implemented. The success of the early agriculture-led reforms also increased the demand for non-agricultural goods and released a surplus of labor and capital into the rural non-farm sector. As the rural non-farm economy thrived, it provided farmers and rural areas with an additional investment source outside agriculture and its allied sectors, and it put pressure on the urban economy to reform as well, since non-farm enterprises in rural areas became more competitive than SOEs. These successes triggered macroeconomic reforms and also favored the opening up of the economy and the adoption of measures such as the special economic zones to increase foreign investment.

1.4. Information Biases

For policymakers to make evidence-based decisions, it is key to have information on the payoffs and risks of different policy options. While a large population like China's is likely to produce many good ideas and solutions to problems, its size also makes it more difficult to aggregate the scattered ideas and feed them back to the policymakers. In a non-democratic society, the problem of asymmetric information may be particularly serious.

Due to China's vast size and uniquely centralized governance structure, there is a huge information asymmetry between the top policy-makers and people on the ground. The case studies illustrate different ways to reduce the information asymmetry. First of all, it is important that policymakers at the top realize that they are likely to be subject to information bias (as in the "emperor's new clothes"). In China's case, as documented by Dr. Luo, after the Cultural Revolution, the top leaders were extremely willing to look for the best ideas on the ground. Due to lack of other communication channels, think tanks (such as the Rural Development Research Center led by Mr. Du) played a key role in the initial reform period by searching for best practices, piloting policy experiments, and analyzing and feeding recommendations back to the Chinese leadership. At the time, there was also an atmosphere of tolerating different views. The leadership had de-politicized collective learning, as described in Chapter 3 by Luo Xiaopeng. This open debate in the now famous Moganshan Conference in 1984 stimulated the invention of the idea of the dual-track pricing. Facing large uncertainties in policy reform, open policy discussions can play a key role in expanding the choice set and increasing the likelihood of finding best solutions.

Secondly, for a large country such as China, each region may face different binding constraints, and it is hard to come up with a one-size-fits-all strategy. Under this circumstance, giving local governments freedom to explore the best solutions to their local binding constraints becomes crucially important in innovations. As shown in Zhu Kangdui's case study, the success of the Wenzhou model of industrial privatization lies largely in its continuous experimentation and innovations which were implicitly supported or at least not opposed by the central government. In the formulation of migration policies, as described by Professor Cai Fang in Chapter 4, the central government encouraged local governments to try different reform measures. One virtue of China's vast size is that, as long as experimentation is allowed, the chance of finding a best solution to challenging problems is quite high. Moreover, the best practice has strong externalities. Not only does it have a huge demonstration effect for other regions, but it can also be scaled up. Both the Wenzhou model and village election case studies highlight this point.

1.5. Reducing Resistance to Reform

Even if a good reform measure has been identified, reformers still need an effective strategy to reduce political resistance. Faced with a planned reform, some vested interest groups may perceive a loss as a result of it. A successful reform strategy should try to reduce opponents' perceived risks and protect their interests, at least in the short run.

Take the household responsibility system (HRS) as an example. Its principle is that individual households can claim the balance after fulfilling the grain quota to both the state and collective units. Under this arrangement, the rent claim rights on agriculture products belong to peasants. The key condition is that farmers must meet the compulsory quota to the state before selling the extra production to the market. Because peasants could possess the entire balance after fulfilling the state quota, their enthusiasm for production dramatically increased. The improved incentive system immediately resulted in the full utilization of the long-term investments by the state in agricultural research and development, irrigation, and other infrastructure.

While with hindsight it is clear that the design of the HRS was a great success, most province governors opposed it in the beginning, on ideological grounds. As a response, the reformers proposed to conduct the HRS pilots in the most remote provinces. In doing so, either the success or failure of the pilots would not affect other richer provinces which perceived higher risk in the HRS. Most governors agreed with the idea of pilots in remote provinces. In the next year, the pilots showed powerfully that the HRS greatly improved agricultural productivity while its risk was minimal. With the new information on payoffs and risks, almost all the provincial governors reversed their opposition in favor of the HRS in the next year. The HRS was quickly scaled up nationwide.

Prior to reform, in the hierarchical property right and entitlement system, urban sectors, particularly SOEs under the control of the central, provincial, and municipal governments, enjoyed privileged access to a variety of scarce materials and capital goods through quotas. There were few quotas, however, for other lower-level SOEs and even fewer for collectively-owned enterprises. The dual pricing system, as described by Luo Xiaopeng, allowed SOEs to sell unused input quota at market price to township and village enterprises (TVEs) which were outside the command economy. Such exchanges not only protected the original privileges of higher ranking entitlements, but also presented TVEs with opportunities to access industrial inputs via market channels and to participate in the market economy. In other words, the dual pricing system provided a functional pricing mechanism for rent sharing through both hierarchical and market systems. Because the dual-price reform initially did not have a negative impact on the SOEs' entitled planned quota, resistance to the reform was muted. Over time, as the private sector grew rapidly and the market price and planned price converged, the dual-track was eventually unified into a single-track or market price.

1.6. Institutions and Capacity

Finally, any reform must be built upon existing institutions and capacity. It is hard to establish new institutions from scratch. Local people usually have much better tacit knowledge on the strengths and weaknesses of their own institutions. Therefore, they are more likely to have better ideas to engineer institutional change than an outsider. No doubt, the knowledge stock from the outside world is extremely useful — but the key is how to facilitate the exchange between external knowledge and indigenous knowledge to solve local problems. Having the capacity to learn and adapt to changing environments is an essential condition for the success of any reform. Undoubtedly, China has a rather strong top-down governmental structure. Once a decision is made, the speed of implementation is much faster than in many democratic countries. International observers have been struck by the efficiency which with China "gets things done", once priorities are recognized. For example, policies on agricultural development, rural industrialization, migration, the control of SARS, HIV/AIDS prevention and harm reduction, and currently the responses to the 2008–2009 financial crisis have been rapidly implemented at the local level.

The top leadership's commitment to reform also played a key role in pushing reform forward. In particular, Mr. Deng Xiaoping advocated a pragmatic approach for reform by relying on empirical evidence and experience on the ground rather than on dogmatic beliefs from textbooks. It was the top leaders who granted wide space for local governments to experiment. Zhejiang Province's bold experiment of abolishing rural taxation proved that the benefits of the reform far outweighed the costs. As a result, this policy was quickly scaled up (Chapter 8). Certainly, the strength of civil service ensured the implementation of various reforms (Ravallion, 2007).

Cai Fang's case study on migration policy (Chapter 4) shows the importance of adaptive efficiency and tacit knowledge. In the planned economic era, China implemented a strict migration policy, the so-called *Hukou* (household registration system), restricting people to their natal places. The government was afraid that a sudden abolishment of the *Hukou* system could lead to massive inflows to cities and create slums. With this concern, governments took a gradual approach to lessen the control on human mobility. Initially, it allowed farmers to go to cities to sell agricultural products, such as vegetables and fruits. Next, the food coupon, which permitted one to purchase grain and other food products from certain locations, was abolished so that people could buy grain at the market price anywhere. This enabled many farmers to live in cities. In response to the death of a college student who was beaten to death for lacking an identification card in Guangzhou, the central government passed a law to prohibit law enforcement from checking people's ID and other paperwork on the street. This made migration much easier than before. As more and more rural people work in the cities, urban residents are gradually finding that they cannot live without the necessary services provided by the rural people. Recently, many local governments have abolished the *Hukou* system, and since the last National

Party Congress migrant workers have become represented in national politics.

Thus, the case studies in this volume show that learning by experimentation is a key feature of China's reform process. While there is justifiably a lot of excitement about what China has achieved, the success has also created a range of problems such as access to healthcare and basic education in the countryside, the environmental costs of development policies, and groundwater pollution in agriculture.

As China has accumulated huge foreign reserves and fiscal revenues, policymakers may become overconfident about their contribution to the economy's success. The recent policy debates indeed show an increasing confidence, and China seems to be among the few countries able to manage the current financial crisis even though growth rates have dropped greatly in China too. Under this complacency, one is more likely to make centralized decisions, neglecting the wisdom from local levels and the virtues of experimentation. The reform stories presented in this book highlight the virtue of pragmatism and experimentation in the reform process. To overcome emerging challenges, it is important that policymakers continue to focus on innovations from local levels with a pragmatic attitude.

1.7. Are There Lessons for Other Countries?

Leaders from developing countries, notably Africa, have shown great interest in China's economic success and record of poverty reduction. Development scholars have noted that China's rise challenges the fundamentals of development theory. We return to this question in the last chapter of this volume, with a review of the growing literature on the subject and a consideration of the way in which policy learning occurs.

In conclusion to this introduction, we highlight that such lessons for others are not easily drawn. This is not only because the context of China is so different from that of most other countries. The key to China's success and ways in which it addresses emerging challenges is clearly the pragmatism and understanding that solutions need to be based in local contexts, combined with a political drive to promote reforms and the space given — by necessity or otherwise — to local experimentation.

The international community is gradually moving away from an understanding that China's reforms are still "partial", to a better empirical understanding of how the reforms took place, how and why they were initiated, and what successes and challenges emerged as a result. We hope that the contributions in this volume make a modest contribution to understanding China's development path, and thus also enrich the global development debate.

References

Dollar, David (2007). "Learning from China: What Works and What Doesn't," memo, World Bank.

Duflo, Esher (2005). "Field Experiments in Development Economics," Bureau for Research in Economic Analysis of Development Policy Paper No. 12.

Fan, Shenggen, Linxiu Zhang and Xiaobo Zhang (2004). "Reform, Investment and Poverty in Rural China," *Economic Development and Cultural Change*, 52(2): 395–422.

Gulati, Ashok and Shenggen Fan (2007). *The Dragon and the Elephant: Agricultural and Rural Reforms in China and India.* Johns Hopkins Press.

Hofman, Bert and Jinglian Wu (2007). "Explaining China's Development and Reforms," Growth Commission Paper.

Lin, Justin Yifu (2007). "Development and Transition: Idea, Strategy and Viability," The Marshall Lectures for 2007–2008, October 31 and November 1, Cambridge University.

Murphy, Kevin M., Andrei Schleifer and Robert W. Vishny (1992). "The Transition to a Market Economy: Pitfalls of Partial Reform," *The Quarterly Journal of Economics*, 107(3): 889–906.

North, Douglass C. (2001). "Needed: A Theory of Change," in *Frontiers of Development Economics: The Future in Perspective*, Meier, Gerald M. and Joseph E. Stiglitz (eds.), p. 491. New York: Oxford University Press.

North, Douglas (2005). *Understanding the Process of Economic Change.* New Jersey: Princeton University Press.

Qian, Yingyi (2003). "How Reform Worked in China," in *In Search of Prosperity: Analytic Narratives on Economic Growth*, Rodrik, Dani (ed.), pp. 297–333. Princeton and Oxford: Princeton University Press.

Ravallion, Martin (2007). "Are There Any Lessons for Africa from China's Success against Poverty?" World Bank Research Working Paper.

Ravallion, Martin and Shaohua Chen (2007). "China's (Uneven) Progress against Poverty," *Journal of Development Economics*, 82(1): 1–42.

Rodrik, Dani (1996). "Understanding Economic Policy Reform," *Journal of Economic Literature*, 34(1): 9–41.

Rodrik, Dani (2004). "Industrial Policy for the Twenty-First Century," CEPR Discussion Paper 4767.

Summers, Lawrence (2007). "The Rise of Asia and the Global Economy," *Research Monitor* (the bi-annual newsletter of the Global Development Network), Special Issue: 4–5.

Wang, Yan (2005). "Development as a Process of Learning and Innovation: Lessons from China," in *Reducing Poverty on a Global Scale: Learning and Innovating for Development — Findings from the Shanghai Global Learning Objective*, Moreno-Dodson, Blanca (ed.), Chapter 3. Washington, DC: The World Bank.

Yao, Yang (2007). "The Chinese Land Tenure System: Practice and Perspectives," in *The Dragon and the Elephant: Agricultural and Rural Reforms in China and India*, Gulati, Ashok and Shenggen Fan (eds.), pp. 49–70. Johns Hopkins Press.

Zhang, Linxiu, Scott Rozelle and Jikun Huang (2007). "Poverty Alleviation in China: Success and Lessons," in *The Dragon and the Elephant: Agricultural and Rural Reforms in China and India*, Gulati, Ashok and Shenggen Fan (eds.), pp. 425–439. Johns Hopkins Press.

Zhang, Xiaobo and Xiaopeng Luo (2007). "How to Make Pro-Poor Policy Work? Lessons from China's Rural Reform," paper at the Global Development Network Conference, Beijing, January 14–16, 2007.

CHAPTER 2

THE COURSE OF CHINA'S RURAL REFORM

Du Runsheng*

2.1. Reform Facilitated by Crisis

For more than 20 years after the victory of the Chinese Revolution, radicalism was ascendant and private ownership of land was illegal. The peasantry became estranged from the land, so that when the Cultural Revolution ended, China's economy had been placed in difficulty and an agricultural crisis was induced. The population had grown and food was in short supply. Per capita grain production never averaged much above 300 kg. Of the 800 million peasants, 250 million were impoverished. The nation as a whole could not achieve self-sufficiency in grain and required massive imports.

A turning point took place in 1978 with the Third Plenum of the 11th Central Committee of the CCP, which reestablished emancipation of the

---

* Du Runsheng held the post of Secretary-General, Rural Work Department, in the Chinese Communist Party (CCP) Central Committee party at the time the nation was founded. Concurrently he was deputy director of the Agriculture and Forestry Department of the State Council. After the Third Plenum of the 11th Central Committee of the CCP (1978), he held the post of director, Rural Policy of the CCP Central Committee, and director of the Rural Department, Research Center for Rural Development (RCRD), State Council, where he was mainly responsible for China's rural economic reforms and development policy research. Du was often asked by the leadership to draft rural-related policy documents for the Central Committee of the CCP and the State Council. He worked in particular on the drafting of "No. 1 Documents", which were issued continuously for five years by the CCP Central Committee, and which made outstanding theoretical and practical contributions, deepening rural economic reform and setting up the rural household contract responsibility system that advanced the market reform of the rural economy.

mind, the intellectual approach of seeking truth from facts, and the materialist philosophy proposition that practice is the sole standard of truth. It acknowledged that socialism means development of the productive forces, moving together towards wealth. The policy of making class struggle the key link was abolished, and the focus of Party work shifted to modernization. All of these changes liberated people from the previous ideological and institutional environment, providing the possibility for founding a new environment and new institutions.

During the 30 years following the founding of the nation, an unfair pattern of holding resources had arisen, fostering the rise of vested interests. These interests tended to be conservative, holding back reform in the name of socialist ownership. The system itself suffered from inertia. Institutional economics speaks of institutional "path dependencies". The Chinese system had been following its accustomed path for a long time, and these conservative interests wanted to keep following it. They feared that order would fall into chaos if they left the old track. The equation of socialism with the system of public ownership, which had been in existence for so long, was decisive. Then, peasants in Yongjia County in the region of Wenzhou, Zhejiang, and in Fengyang County, Anhui, seeking to end their food shortages, implemented a policy of contracting collective land to families. Because it violated what Mao Zedong had advocated, contracted production operated by peasant households had been a forbidden practice.

When I first proposed the household responsibility system (HRS), I was criticized as follows: Chairman Mao had been dead only a few years. Supporting the HRS, a system he opposed, meant forsaking his principles. This was the severe environment that reform faced at first. Our support of the HRS, of institutional innovation, and of transformation of the agents of the rural microeconomy would inevitably involve adjusting a number of interests. To avoid risks, it was necessary to carry out trials first. Also, the HRS could not move ahead on its own; it had to do so in connection with other institutions, and be realized in the course of reforming the institutional environment as a whole. But this institutional reform was not something that could be accomplished in one fell swoop. To carry out reform, a strategy of gradual advance was unavoidable.

2.2. The Cause of Reform Must Strive to Reduce Resistance

All land and labor in China were held by the hundreds of thousands of People's Communes. Upon its appearance, the HRS policy shook the People's Communes to the core. This assault on communal ownership was sure to encounter enormous resistance. The greater the impact, the greater this resistance would be. Hence, to promote the HRS and ward off its early demise, resistance to it had to be reduced as much as possible and facilitation boosted.

Three measures to reduce resistance were conceived. First, the reform would not initially call for abandoning the People's Communes, but rather would implement a production responsibility system within them. This approach enabled many who would have opposed the change to accept it.

Second, the responsibility system could take a number of forms, among which the populace could choose. One did not impose one's own subjective preference on the populace but respected its choice. Later, it seemed that the masses were bent on choosing the household contract form. A popular saying to explain the system was, "Household contract — keep straight on and don't turn back, hand over enough to the state, keep enough in the collective; whatever is left over is your own." The ideas were easy to understand, and the interest allocations were clear. The idea of letting the populace choose for itself also paid off in terms of checking the feasibility of reformers' initial positions.

Third, the reform began in a limited region, where it received popular support, and then widened step by step. In the spring of 1979, the newly established National Agriculture Commission convened a conference with the seven major agricultural provinces in Beijing's Chongwenmen Hotel to discuss the responsibility system issue. Anhui was already experimenting with the HRS. But five of the seven provinces at the meeting disagreed with Anhui's approach. When CCP General Secretary Hua Guofeng held a Politburo meeting to hear the report, he spoke of how Hunan villagers exchanged labor to help each other every sowing or harvest season, and he supported persisting with the collective approach. But he expressed approval for solitary households in mountainous areas, for whom collective activities were difficult, to adopt the HRS. The Central Committee relayed the "Summary of Discussions on Rural Work

Questions" from the National Agriculture Commission's party group, which continued to stipulate that "there will be no HRS" and "there will be no dividing the land to go it alone." Although people in areas with solitary households were not given explicit permission in the document to carry out the HRS, it was not forbidden either; they would not be subject to criticism and struggle or corrected coercively. Once transmitted, the authorization of this document by Hua Guofeng opened a small window for the HRS.[1]

In 1980 the window grew wider. At that time, those regions with severe rural poverty had become a heavy burden on the state. More provinces were moving from grain self-sufficiency to grain deficits, and fewer provinces had grain surpluses. The state held a long-term planning conference, and Yao Yilin, then director of the State Planning Commission, raised with me the question of how to reduce the problem of food shortages in impoverished regions. I suggested trying the HRS. If the peasants could solve the food problem themselves, they would no longer depend on purchased grain. Once land was contracted to a farmer, he could depend on his own land for food. Yao Yilin thought this made sense and reported as such to Deng Xiaoping, who agreed and declared, "Impoverished regions are allowed to carry out the HRS. If it turns out to be mistaken and they come back in, it's nothing special. Rich regions that have enough to eat do not need to start right away."

In 1980, after the central leadership was reorganized on a collective basis, the top central leaders, including Deng Xiaoping and Hu Yaobang, consistently supported allowing different areas to adopt different forms of the agricultural production responsibility system. It was then proposed to divide them into three types of areas: impoverished areas would carry out the HRS; advanced areas would adopt specialized contracts with wages linked to output; and intermediate regions could freely choose. In the autumn of 1980, the top leadership held a conference of Party Committee First Secretaries of major provinces and cities to discuss the responsibility

---

[1] For more information about this period, see Kathleen Hartford, "Socialist Agriculture Is Dead, Long Live Socialist Agriculture! Organizational Transformations in Rural China," in Elizabeth J. Perry and Christine Wong, eds., *The Political Economy of Reform in Post-Mao China* (Cambridge, MA: Harvard University Press, 1985).

system, producing "No. 75 Document", namely "Some Problems in Further Strengthening and Improving the Agricultural Production Responsibility System."[2] The tests proved instantly effective. By the second year the impoverished areas had food to eat, and other areas too saw increased production. These facts convinced the leaders and opened the way for rural reform.

2.3. The Central Committee's Five "No. 1 Documents"

In late 1981, the Central Committee held a national conference on rural work. Soon after the meeting, the Central Committee's "No. 1 Document" for 1982 (namely the conference summary) was drafted and officially affirmed that management of the land by peasant households under the contract system would replace unified collective management by the People's Communes. HRS, after 30 years of being proscribed, henceforth became central government policy. Reactions from the populace and cadres were excellent. Party Secretary Hu Yaobang said that the rural work document should again be placed "No. 1" the next year. For the next five years, the Central Committee's "No. 1 Documents" were all devoted to agricultural issues; topics for investigation were arranged early in the year, the findings were summarized in the autumn, and the document drafted in the winter and sent out early in the next year.

The first "No. 1 Document", issued in 1982, pointed out that HRS was a legitimate policy reform that had been warmly welcomed by the populace and taken up nationally. This reform was the self-perfection of the socialist system; it was different from the private farming of the past and was not something to oppose, like capitalism. Public ownership of land and other means of production would be unchanged for a long time to come, as would the responsibility system. At the time peasants in many regions were worried, given that rural policy had been very changeable in the past (the Guangdong peasants were afraid of "relaxation in the first year, tightening up in the second, eating the words in the third"). They were also concerned that it was an "expedient measure". The phrase "unchanged for a long time" therefore had the greatest impact on people's

---

[2] See http://news.xinhuanet.com/ziliao/2005-02/04/content_2547020.htm.

minds, and it was said that the "No. 1 Document" gave the peasants a "sedative".

Another main point of the document was its respect for people's choice: the populace was allowed to choose freely to suit different areas and conditions. Why was it not imposed as a unified solution? As recognized by institutional economics, forming a stable system must be a process in which the populace chooses for itself. This process includes different sides in mutual dialogue leading to coordination and integration, according to the requirements of the interests and political pursuits of each side. Given that the Party wanted to give the populace a free choice, we did not need to turn this practice into state law for the time being. We had to treat the law as the outcome of a social choice and eventually provide legal guarantees in the form of law. We needed to allocate one or two years to promote this change in society, and later it would become a national law. Such a process would help the country absorb the advantages of both public ownership and individual management. The document also proposed adjusting the field of distribution, bringing unified purchasing and marketing within the reform agenda, and continuing the reform of the price system at a steady pace. It also re-endorsed the development diversified management of the rural economy and enterprises run by communes and production brigades. It proposed the new concept of specialized households, encouraging individuals and the private sector to engage in specialization and growth and setting up a professional division of labor. For more than 20 years, long-distance trading had been forbidden, as were private operated or contractual procurement, in essence restricting the circulation of resources. The first "No. 1 Document" was rich in content, but more importantly, it abolished the forbidden area of HRS in the name of the Central Committee. When delivered to the Central Committee leaders for examination and approval, Deng Xiaoping said after reading it: "I completely agree." Chen Yun told his secretary to make a phone call, saying, "I've read this document. It's fine and will be supported by the cadres and people."

After its release, HRS spread nationwide, liberating both land and labor. In 1978, China's grain yield was approximately 300 billion kg. Over 20 years of collectivization, the state had purchased between 30 and 35 billion kg of grain annually. The latitude for state procurement was so small that even if the state increased procurement by only 10 percent, it would not be able to meet its grain rations. With the system reform, grain output increased to 400 billion kg by 1984. At the same time, the value of gross agricultural output grew by 68 percent and the peasants' average income per person grew 166 percent. This achievement, which attracted worldwide attention, finally convinced cadres who had held opposing views and unified the way people thought.

Closely following this reform, the comparative advantage of plentiful labor was enhanced by allowing the countryside to establish industry and commerce. The sudden appearance of new rural enterprises, together with foreign and private firms, formed a large non-state economic bloc, rectifying the overly simplified economic form that was a weakness of the public ownership system, and opening huge new sources for growth in peasant incomes. These changes inspired confidence and impelled economic reform throughout the nation.

The 12th National Party Congress was held in September 1982. In his Work Report, Hu Yaobang stated on behalf of the Central Committee that the various forms of the production responsibility system established in recent years in the countryside had liberated the productive forces and needed to be maintained for a long time. They could only be gradually improved on the basis of people's practical experience; in no way should they be rashly changed against the wishes of the people, nor should they be reversed, he said. Reporting to the 5th National People's Congress on behalf of the State Council, Premier Zhao Ziyang reaffirmed that the output-linked contract system "effectively displays the superiority of the socialist economic system in rural China in the present stage".

In that same year, to consolidate and expand on the achievements of rural reform, in a speech written for the 12th National Party Congress on "Historical Shift in Rural Work", I gave an account of how household output contracting and household work contracting could embody the unification of public and private benefits and of near-term development and the distant goal of modernization. I said that the peasants required the present policies to be stabilized so that they could do well for several years and that I hoped the Party and government could accept this request. It would help the peasants to escape the difficulties of their self-sufficient economy, by allowing them to produce commodities to increase their cash income and to seek their own all-round development.

I gave another speech entitled "Policy Must Continue to Bring Things to Life". While visiting Fujian, I toured a chicken hatchery where 14 people had each invested 2,000 yuan. The workshop spanned 100 square meters and hatched 1.2 million chickens annually. Nearby there was a state farm, also with a chicken hatchery, where the state had invested several hundred thousand yuan, but hatched only 500,000 chickens per year. I used what I had seen to show that at China's stage of economic development, keeping up economic growth and achieving overall benefits would be very difficult if investment depended only on the government (central, or town and village) and if making a living depended on compensation according to work alone in this kind of simplified economic structure.

I argued for a basic structure of coexistence of a variety of economic forms, with public ownership in charge. I also argued for permitting distribution according to their work. That is, people should receive dividends according to the capital, land, and technology invested, in order to encourage them to increase savings and investment to make up for the shortage of state investment. I raised these issues in view of some disagreements from below about, for example, whether to allow private purchase of tractors and cars, operation of long-distance transport, and formation of partnerships to build fishponds with dividends paid according to stock held.

Here is an anecdote: A leading cadre in Huber once drove after a private tractor driven by a peasant. When he caught up with him, he blamed the peasant, saying, "If I hadn't been chasing you in a car, you might have gotten away." The peasant replied, "Right! You know a car is faster than a tractor, I know a tractor is faster than an ox cart — so how come you can buy a car, but I can't buy a tractor?" The leading cadre couldn't answer. Party and government cadres claimed that tractors were producer goods, so they could only be publicly owned and could not be bought privately. Hence, the "No. 1 Document" for 1983 (namely "Some Issues in Current Rural Economic Policy") proposed a further goal to strive for: the "Two Shifts and Three Bits". The two shifts were to shift agriculture from economic whole or part self-sufficiency to comparatively large-scale commodity production, and to shift from traditional to modern agriculture. All levels of leading cadres in the Party and various government departments were supposed to make every effort to achieve the three "bits" — a bit more liberation of ideas, a bit bolder reform, and a bit more realistic attitude — to help speed up the two shifts.

In 1983 the pace of rural reform accelerated, and the changes it caused in economic life became more obvious. Household contracting spread to virtually all villages, and rural workers were liberated from their state of being left unused as the approaches to commodity production were actively expanded. The marketed proportion of agriculture grew from the 51.5 percent of previous years to 59.9 percent. Output value reached 275.3 billion yuan, an increase of 129.9 billion yuan, or 90 percent, over 1978 levels.

In 1984 we proposed freeing up channels for trade so that competition could boost development. Whereas the first two "No. 1 Documents" had tried to solve problems of the micro-management of agriculture and rural industry and commerce, in this case the target was fostering market mechanisms.

Developing commodity production requires free trade and fluid factors of production like capital, land, and labor, and these ideas came into conflict with government policy. In the preceding 20 years, a system of unified and forced state purchases had been carried out in the countryside. Besides mandatory state purchase of three items (grain, cotton and oil), this system also applied to another 132 items, including live pigs, eggs, sugar, silk thread, silkworm cocoons, yellow bluish dogbane, flue-cured tobacco and aquatic products, which were purchased by assignment (that is, purchased amounts were subject to quotas, but at a relatively fair market price). It included virtually all agricultural supplementary and local products. For many items purchased by assignment, the quantity purchased accounted for more than 90 percent of the ultimate output. In fact, rural product transactions were monopolized by the public sector. The mobility of capital, land, and labor was institutionally limited by public ownership of the means of production and by the organizational institution of People's Communes, as well as by enforced separation of city and countryside.

Following a thorough investigation, the Central Committee Rural Policy Research Department, which I directed, put together a written suggestion proposing a Central Secretariat Conference to discuss this problem. Besides describing the situation, we stated that to help rural people develop commodity production and climb out of poverty, the rural economy urgently required relaxation of government monopolies, controls, and other regulations that had formed over many years and that were preventing peasants from entering the market. Specifically, we suggested the following: (1) the period of land contracts should be extended to 15 years, during which paid transfer of land use rights should be permitted; (2) the free flow of rural private funds should be allowed, combining the cooperative joint stock to earn dividends; (3) the peasants should be allowed to go to the cities to seek work, do business and run enterprises, and be responsible for procuring their own grain ration at market prices; (4) private individuals should be allowed to run enterprises and hire staff and management; and (5) state-operated businesses and state-operated supply and marketing cooperatives should gradually open up to market transactions, withdraw from their market monopolies, change their form of service, and return supply and marketing cooperatives to private operation.

Most of the leading comrades in attendance expressed support. Of the proposals, items 1, 2 and 3 passed without objection. Item 5 called for a reform of trade, marketing and sales and financial agencies to occur all together with reconsideration of the state monopoly on purchase and sales of grain. In the first step toward item 5, nearly all mandatory purchases were abolished, with only the grain, cotton, and oil monopolies retained. On the question of employees in item 4, Hu Qiaomu raised the issue of how to deal with Party members who were also employers. After discussion there was still no consensus, and a conclusion proved hard to reach. It was agreed by all that issues that were unclear could be laid aside for later review and handling. This was also a new policy. In the past, firms of eight or fewer employees were ruled not to be capitalist, whereas trials were implemented for firms of more than eight persons. After the meeting Deng Xiaoping was asked for instructions, and he said, "Don't be eager to set limits. Look at it again after three years." All of these principles were to form the contents of the "No. 1 Document" for 1984.

In 1985 the tasks were to adjust production structure and abolish unified purchasing and marketing. With simultaneous reform of the rural economy's microeconomic management agencies and macroeconomic market environment, China had seen fast growth of agricultural production in 1984. Regarding food grain, that topmost of top priorities, the situation changed from "when you hold grain, your heart feels no pain" to "grain supplies are higher, but hard to find buyers." Following an observation trip to the country with Hu Yaobang, I concluded that the cheapness of grain was hurting the peasantry. On the basis of the existing structure of agricultural production, it was impossible to carry out the task of doubling their income, and a new production structure needed to be built. The main issue was that reform of the agricultural procurement system lagged behind the new requirements for rural economic development, causing various provinces to want to guarantee the area sown to grain and obstructing peasants' arrangements for cultivation to meet the needs of the market. For example, even Hainan proposed being self-sufficient in grain, when in fact planting tropical cash crops, which could be exchanged for imported grain through foreign trade, would have been more worthwhile and more popular with the peasants. Increasing production of some goods for foreign exchange in China's southern region and bringing in grain from outside the region would help the North raise its grain yield and increase its income. Then the two regions could both make the most of local conditions.

Everybody was clear on this principle; the problem was that the monopoly procurement institutions in agriculture had been around for a long time. Inertia was strong, and change was difficult. Fortunately, just then the decision on economic reform emerging from the Third Plenary Session of the 12th Central Committee was favorable toward reconstructing the urban and rural relationship, and reform of the system of unified procurement and adjustments to the industrial structure were made central agenda items of the rural reforms in 1985.

In support of these reforms, we proposed a range of tasks like developing forestry, enhancing transport, supporting rural enterprises, encouraging technological progress, promoting free movement of talented people, enlivening financial markets, perfecting the rural cooperative system, strengthening the building of small cities, and developing the foreign trade-oriented economy. The "No. 1 Document" for 1985 was entitled "On 10 Policies to Further Enliven the Rural Economy".

In 1986 we increased investment in agriculture and adjusted the urban–rural relationship and the industrial–agricultural relationship. In 1985 the uniform grain procurement system had been changed to contract purchasing. Beyond the contract, purchases negotiated with the government changed to market purchases. Of the 132 agricultural products that had been subject to state procurement, only silk thread, medical materials, and tobacco stayed that way, whereas transactions and price setting for the rest were through the market. This reform was originally a thorough one with straightforward goals. Problems arose, however, from raising the grain purchase price without correspondingly raising the price at which it would be sold to city people. Thus, the more grain production increased, the greater the financial subsidy, and massive increases of grain bought at higher prices created a burden too heavy for the state finances to bear. By now, given the state's inertia in maintaining the superior status of urban non-agricultural groups, the state sought to lighten its financial burden by reducing the preferential trade terms for the peasants. The concrete measures taken included a ruling in 1985 to cancel the policy of paying 50 percent more for the grain procured beyond the contract amount and to instead purchase all grain at an increased average price. Although in static terms "three in the morning and four in the evening" is no different to "four in the morning and three in the evening", dynamically, this change greatly weakened the role of the procurement policy in stimulating increased grain production. The comparative advantage of sowing farmland with grain dropped, making the peasants who had already shed their collective fetters unwilling to plant more crops. Peasants in Hebei said planting a *mu* (Chinese unit of land) of wheat was inferior to driving a small flock: the "two types of households" (specialized and primary households in agriculture production) were no match for the burdens caused by the "three households" (referring to three government agencies: industry and commerce administration, taxation, and public security). Many peasants began to diversify their farming activities, start a business, or leave for the city to work.

The injury to the peasants' interests was reflected immediately in reduced supplies of grain and other agricultural products, producing fluctuations in agricultural and especially grain production from then on for years. There were different views at that time about whether this situation was a result of reforms not going far enough or going too far. It was argued that the potential of the HRS had dried up, hence the fluctuation in grain production. Events were to prove this viewpoint wrong.

After developing for several years, supply and demand relations in the national economy changed. Restricted by the Engel's coefficient,[3] the growth of residents' expenditures on food was slow, but market exchanges displayed rising costs for agriculture and the margin from trade dropped. In view of this, rural work deployment at the end of 1985 emphasized "putting the status of agriculture in the national economy straight". The top leadership's "No. 1 Document" for 1986 (namely "On Deployment of Rural Work in 1986") made a commitment to increase investment in agriculture and water facilities and to guarantee a rise in grain production to 450 billion kg, starting with the Seventh Five-Year Plan. Part of the income tax turned in by town and village enterprises was assigned for use in supporting agriculture, stabilizing prices of agricultural inputs like chemical fertilizer, diesel oil, agricultural chemicals, and machinery, and guaranteeing that original subsidies would not vary. These funds have also gone to strengthening technical support of agricultural and rural enterprises and to support grain and export commodities, mainly by introducing new varieties and improving infrastructure. They have also been used to implement the Spark Program, which supports the technological change of rural enterprises by, for instance, designing 100 kinds of complete technical equipments, establishing 500 demonstration enterprises, and promoting them nationally after they yielded practical results, as well as supporting large numbers of technical training and administrative personnel.

In setting out the status and function of agriculture in the national economy, the document stressed agriculture's indispensability as an industry that provides food needed by all human beings. Moreover, in contemporary China, agriculture was the physical foundation that 900 million people depended on for survival and development, and thus was also the economic bastion of the nation's social stability and unity. Yet agriculture was a vulnerable industry, hampered by both natural disasters and market competition. A suitable environment advantageous to its gestation and

---

[3] The ratio of food spending to overall household expenses.

growth, and systems that guaranteed support, needed to be created for it. These were precisely the topics in need of more work after the problem of micro-level agency had been solved by the rural reforms.

2.4. Political Reform Admits No Delay

Further reform of Chinese agriculture involves reform of the urban state-owned economy and of the political system. To use a phrase of that time, regarding China's rural reform, all "cheap" methods had been exhausted. If the deep structure was left untouched, no further progress could be made. For just this reason, the historical mission of the series of "No. 1 Documents" on rural reform was brought to a halt. China's rural reforms were by no means complete but had to seek a path of advancement through the overall reform of the national economy.

Reviewing more than 20 years of rural reform in China, there were no major deviations, only a relapse in understanding initiated by the June 4, 1989 "disturbance". This temporary blockage to understanding was fortunately unable to change the institutional foundation of land management by household contract. All statesmen in power need to treat food security as vital to overall stability. The idea that "first there must be food to eat, next one must build" had therefore become a consensus for a great many leading cadres. In the urban reforms commencing in 1984, market adjustment mechanisms were prepared for introduction. In 1984 the system of price setting by the state changed to a system of price setting by the market. The Central Committee reexamined the decision on this matter at the 1987 Beidaihe meeting. But that year saw poor harvests, price increases, and panic buying in the cities, and people's minds fluctuated. Another factor causing popular dissatisfaction was widespread corruption. Reform of the price mechanism had to be temporarily put aside.

If China had achieved systems of economic and political democracy simultaneously, then when reform led to an essential adjustment of interests, society would have had a stronger mental and physical coping capacity. However, in this area, knowledge is easy, but practice difficult.

In 1992 Deng Xiaoping traveled to the south and gave a series of speeches that prevented reform relapse and made the reform agenda clearer. The new Central Party Committee General Secretary Jiang Zemin visited Anhui, announcing that the family contract system would not change. The central government made the decision that contracts for land would last for 30 years. If needed, this period could be extended further.

There have already been 25 years of rural reform. How will reform deepen, and how will the land system be improved? In particular, how can the family contract system for public land be perfected, maintaining the intimate relationship between peasants and the land, while exploring mutual cooperation and strengthening market competitiveness? These are important questions.

Compared with economic reform, political system reform lags behind. There is a lack of democratic surveillance, which leads to polarization and inequitable distribution. The fruits of reform fall into the hands of the privileged, affecting the income earned by the populace. Moreover, opportunities to own resources are unfairly distributed. The right to control a huge amount of public property is not accompanied by adequate surveillance and democratic participation. In a time of economic transition, there is an inevitable appearance of working for one's own interests under the guise of working for the public, and thus, of the erosion of resources. Political system reform must therefore be initiated, carrying forward democracy, implementing the rule of law, respecting the various rights enjoyed by the people, and guaranteeing that the masses can equitably enjoy the outcomes of economic restructuring. Decision-making regarding important matters touching the interests of the populace should be guaranteed to be public, just, and equitable. Therefore, government functions must be regulated by law and a service government must be established.

CHAPTER 3

COLLECTIVE LEARNING CAPACITY AND CHOICE OF REFORM PATH — THEORETICAL REFLECTIONS ON THE DUAL-TRACK SYSTEM OF PRICE REFORM PROCESS

Luo Xiaopeng*

China's economic reforms of the 1980s achieved a series of major break-throughs, with far-reaching implications for its economic growth. With the aid of fresh theorizing, I have sought for some years to deepen my understanding of the reform process and derive universal significance from my experience as an active participant. This is the latest attempt.

This essay supports the following analysis of China's price reform, with particular regard to the process of formation of the dual-track price system:

The choice of reform path depends largely on society's collective learning capacity, especially that of the elite. The collective learning

* Luo Xiaopeng worked at the Research Center for Rural Development (RCRD) in the 1980s. He was actively involved in rural and price reforms at the time. He was one of the first to propose the now famous dual-track price reform idea. After receiving his Ph.D. from University of Minnesota, he returned to China and has since worked at Guizhou University and Zhejiang University. Currently, he is a professor at the Center for Agricultural and Rural Development in Zhejiang University. The dual-track price reform laid a foundation for China's successful economic transition from a planned to market economy. The seemly heterodox idea has now been widely acclaimed. In this chapter, Dr. Luo provides theoretical reflections on the dual-track system of price reform process.

capacity of the elite depends on its value rationality, its stock of knowledge and its communicative rationality (Habermas, 1985). The collective environmental resilience of a social elite — what North calls its collective "adoptive efficiency" (North, 2005) — is determined by the combination of these three elements.

The breakthroughs in reform in China in the early 1980s were nurtured by a return to rationality in Chinese society induced by the comprehensive crisis of the Cultural Revolution, and the post-Mao political atmosphere of public rationality. In this environment, even though theoretical knowledge was quite impoverished in the country, the vision of political leaders and communication within the elite reached high levels of rationality, thereby overcoming worries the advantaged classes had about changing things, and arousing local leaders, the disadvantaged classes, and above all the enthusiasm of young intellectuals to reform and innovate, and forming an irreversible situation of reform. Forming and carrying through the dual-track price reform idea was but one of many important results of rational communication within the Chinese elite in the early reform period.

Due to their political culture and institutions, however, rational communication within the Chinese elite who lack self-consciousness is fragile. Later in the reform process, there are inevitably divisions of interest and of trust within the strata, such that the choice of reform path is increasingly constrained by the personal cognitive ability of the policymakers and advantaged interest groups.

In this era of globalization, the value rationality (Weber's *wertrationalität*) and the stock of knowledge are tremendously impacted by exogenous forces. The avoidance of disastrous path choices for a society comes to rely, to an unprecedented extent, on enhancing collective cognitive ability of society as a whole through communicative rationality.

This paper consists of three main sections. The first section reflects on the larger environment in which the idea of the dual-track price reform was formed; the core of this discussion is the relation between crisis and reform. The second section reflects on the process of formation and realization of the dual-track price system reform concept; the core of this discussion is the influence of collective cognitive ability on the choice of reform path. The third section reflects on the influence of the dual-track price system reform path on China's economic and political development, so as to further discuss the choice of reform path and collective learning, especially its relationship with communicative rationality.

3.1. Crisis and Reform: How the Cultural Revolution Catastrophe Provided an Opportunity for China's Reform

3.1.1. *Reform and perceived risk*

Without the disaster of the Cultural Revolution, there would have been no reform in China — this is a consensus view among many who experienced this historical period. How, though, was the Cultural Revolution catastrophe able to bring China the opportunity for reform? We know that historically many successful reforms were prompted by crisis and disaster, but not all crises and disasters lead to successful reform. What then is the relationship between crisis and reform?

Reform is dominated by change in the upper social strata, thus differing from social change led by the lower strata. The difficulty with social change led by the powerful is that the upper echelons who are advantaged in the existing order fear losing their privileges, hence it is difficult for them to come to a consensus on reform. Hence, promoting consensus on reform is a major function of crisis. However, even if the crisis leads to consensus on the need for reform, it may not be able to produce a consensus on how this should take place. Many crisis-induced reforms are unsuccessful for this very reason.

China achieved major breakthroughs in the late 1970s shortly after the reforms were launched, above all with household contracting, the tremendous success of which stunned the world. Some unintended aspects of household contracting are thought-provoking, and embody truths worth going into in depth. At the start of reform, it was generally considered to be too radical and dangerous, and hence was excluded from policy choices; but it was precisely this reform that was within a few years to become the leading policy. Why was this? More interesting is why this reform was not as terrible as many had originally imagined, but benefited almost everyone — most of all, even some who had initially opposed it. Most thought-provoking of all is: given that, as facts have proven, this reform initiative was a very good Pareto optimization, why were so many people against it? What kind of reform strategy was it that did not allow these initial opponents to prevent change, so that China's reform embarked on a different path?

Based on this historical experience, I distilled a concept of the perceived risk of reform. While social crisis makes the powerful strata recognize the need for reform, they are all aware of the riskiness of reform, with not only political risk to themselves, but public risk of social disorder. The experience of the household contracting reform shows that there are not only problems in judging how big the risks of reform are, but also problems in identifying which risks are genuine. Misjudgment of the risks of reform by the powerful strata will have a major impact on the choice of reform path. The concept of perceived risk helps illustrate this problem.

"Perceived risk of reform" refers to an apparent but unreal risk perceived by the powerful strata, who mistake reform initiatives that are essentially Pareto-improving as risky. Due to learning limitations, some reforms later proven to deliver tremendous Pareto improvements (in particular, some that enhance the rights of the vulnerable strata so as to promote improvements to the welfare of society as a whole) were, in the view of some in the powerful class strata, *ex ante* unacceptably risky in personal and public terms; they therefore were willing to devote a lot of political resources to stop these reforms from being realized. When they did this (whether or not it ultimately came to anything), any such initiative would have lost the potential Pareto-optimal nature it originally had, because as far as the opposition was concerned, the issue was not only that they had paid a very high price to stop the reform, but that an unacceptable price would have to be paid for any change in their position. Historically, due to the cognitive limitations of the powerful strata and irreversibilities in the political process, many societies lose opportunities for significant Pareto improvements. There have been many regrettable examples in the course of China's modernization.

3.1.2. *The Cultural Revolution raised the collective rationality of Chinese society*

How then was China, fresh from the disasters and crises of the Cultural Revolution, able to seize a series of opportunities for major reform to bring about a historic leap in economic development? My explanation is that while bringing calamity, the Cultural Revolution also boosted the collective learning capacity of Chinese society. Mao Zedong plunged both the elite and populace into a huge, irrational game of public politics, in which virtually everyone involuntarily became participants and victims. Shared experience of this unprecedented, frenzied, public, common political game brought China's political and intellectual elites an uncommon opportunity for collective reflection, thus greatly improving collective rationality of Chinese society.

As many have recognized, the prime element forming collective rationality is value rationality, which is also what North calls the belief system (North, 2005). The greatest contribution the Cultural Revolution made to Chinese society's return to value rationality lay in that this common experience fundamentally shook the legitimacy of political persecution. The announcement by the historic Third Plenum of the 13th Central Committee that it would abandon (the Maoist policy of) treating class struggle as the key link, and shift to taking economic construction as the center, was an important sign of this return.

A peculiar political situation emerged in China following the expulsion of the Gang of Four from the political arena. On the one hand, the romantic enthusiasm for public politics inspired by the Cultural Revolution still survived in the popular memory, especially among the youth; on the other hand, this spontaneous public politics, lacking the support and protection of both the rule of law and democratic institutions, had, due to lessons learnt from the Cultural Revolution, enhanced rationality. High-level politics and public opinion were hence brought into benign interaction, not only supporting the return to the center of power of veteran cadres who had been humiliated in the Cultural Revolution, but also inspiring in these former revolutionaries an ambition for and confidence in reform, and creating a political atmosphere of public rationality rare in the history of China.

This rare spontaneous public rationality was expressed not only in widespread public concern for politics and eagerness to participate, but especially within the power-holding strata, the civil elites, and in open public exchanges between the two. Many young people concerned with public politics not only enjoyed unprecedented freedom of communication, but could frankly exchange political views among themselves.

It is clear in retrospect that spontaneous "public rationality" in such a particular historical context lacked both a solid social foundation and theoretical self-awareness, and hence was extremely fragile. The enthusiasm for public politics of people, especially the youth, might at some time come into conflict with the existing power structure and system, with tragic results.

The Cultural Revolution turned the political prestige and experience of the older generation of revolutionaries into a resource for reform. A number of outstanding individuals among the older generation of Chinese revolutionaries had been raised to a higher level of political life due to their suffering in the Cultural Revolution. The return to power of such people after undergoing years of frustration meant that their political prestige and experience, earned with the blood of countless lives, not only would not block change, but would in fact act as tremendous social capital for China's reforms.

The issues of historical right and wrong and social reconciliation were addressed by the leaders of the reform (represented by Deng Xiaoping) with great political finesse, speed and simplicity, while wisely and prudently leading the political enthusiasm of the young towards constructive reform.

With his enormous political prestige and fine political wisdom, Deng Xiaoping made irreplaceable contributions to China's reform. His most prominent contribution to the reform lay in his guiding principles and strategies, which greatly increased the collective learning capacity in China in the reform process. Deng Xiaoping's contributions in this regard may be summed up as follows:

He clearly defined reform as a collective learning process. He used the popular expression "feeling our way across the river" to express a learning approach among the leadership that was open, realistic and truth-seeking, and thus encouraged open-ended exploration in reform. It was thanks to the support of this political ideal that the single spark of household contracting in Xiaogang Village could emerge, gain the support of a reform-minded local leader like Wan Li, and eventually develop into a peaceful "decommunizing" revolution.

Deng's injunction to "dispense with polemics" effectively prevented differences in learning (with regard to reform) from being politicized, thus curbing political tendencies that were not conducive to collective learning. Furthermore, his progression from encouraging separate local exploration to encouraging local competition, enabled competition in local governance to become not only a powerful incentive mechanism promoting reform, but also an effective incentive mechanism promoting the nation's collective learning.

3.1.3. *Rational communication defuses perceived risk*

The post-Cultural Revolution elevation of rational communication among China's elite strata was not only expressed in a more rational communication ethics among them, e.g., not lying in meetings. More importantly, the elevation of rational communication helped promote innovations in public politics of great significance for collective action. Such innovations raised the level of rationality of the policy process in China, defusing the perceived risk of reform.

Such innovations in public politics are of great significance for collective action. For example, the appearance of policy think-tanks with autonomous tendencies, especially the recognition of their legitimacy in the policy process, made important contributions to defusing the perceived risk of the reforms. I took part in this process personally, I am proud to say.

The return of "educated youths" to the city after the Cultural Revolution, and especially Deng Xiaoping's dramatic restoration of the college entrance examinations, allowed large numbers of elite youths to return to the political center. Among them were many sons and daughters of senior cadres who, despite having seen some ups and downs in life, had not lost all political ambition; as well as a number of children of civilians who, while having experienced the hazards of Chinese public politics in the Cultural Revolution, were still willing to persevere. Interestingly, the political persecution of the Cultural Revolution had allowed the life trajectories of the two to intersect, and the restoration of order after the Cultural Revolution allowed them to meet up again. This historic gathering of talents inspired the romantic aspirations of a group of people, engendering in them the idea of creating autonomous think-tanks that would serve reform decision-making.

China's opening up and romantic political atmosphere in the early 1980s offered chances of success in small things to these wild imaginations. In the autumn of 1980, China's first officially-funded autonomous think-tank, "China Rural Development Research Group", was formally established. This political innovation was not initially well regarded by many people, until in 1981 the group conducted a systematic field investigation of the Chu county region of Anhui, where household contracting had been in operation for a year. The report carried out what was at the time the most objective, comprehensive and convincing defense of the results of the household contracting reform, and thus promoted consensus on supporting it at the highest levels. From then onwards, the "China Rural Development Research Group" not only won trust at the top levels, but also made it legitimate for other autonomous think-tanks to take part in the policy process — a historic breakthrough in the new Chinese public policy process.

In the political environment of China at that time, how could think-tanks that were trusted by the decision-making strata and autonomous help defuse the perceived risks of reform? According to my personal experience, what mattered most was not that they could come up with some clever ideas, but that they could reduce the communication risks between key decision-makers in the reform policy process, improving the rationality and efficiency of communication in the policy process, and thereby enhancing the efficiency of searching and decision-making in reform. Social change always faces immense uncertainty and contains genuine major risk. Thus, search and decision-making efficiency in the front line of a rapidly changing society often has life-and-death importance.

China is a society that lacks a tradition of local autonomy. Once reunification is achieved, there are serious shortages of legitimate and legal resources for local grassroots collective action. This is because the unified center monopolizes all the resources needed for such action. Such a distribution and structure of the mechanisms and resources for legitimacy of collective action is very negative for learning on the part of society as a whole. Early in the revolution, military blockades forced the CCP to learn how to use the policy experience of different regions to correct central policies while maintaining unity of politics and policy. After seizing power, a continuation of this experience aided the central leadership's search for new paths by making use of exploration by local leaders. In the new political reality, however, moral hazards of communication between central and local governments have greatly increased. Local leaders have found that catering to the likes of central leaders is likely to bring enormous personal returns. This moral hazard was a direct reason leading to the Great Famine of 1959–1960.

In the 1980s, while there were no longer the risks in communication between central and local leaders that had led to the Great Famine, there were still some risks in communication between the central and local reform leaderships. In the non-autonomous "great unification" polity, there is a paradox in using decentralization strategies to search for a reform path: when judging how far a reform can go, the central reform leadership has to first depend on local leaders deciding on the basis of their own judgment in their locality, while the latter must first rely on the overall political judgment of the central leadership. The trouble is, by relying on formal political processes alone, the central and local reform leaderships are unable to achieve full communication. An important reason for this is the moral hazard of information asymmetry.

Think-tanks that are trusted by senior strata, while also somewhat autonomous and independent, are to some extent able to reduce the information asymmetry between the central and local reform leaderships, and thus reduce their communication risks. This helps expand the scope of the reform search, without incurring too much political and policy risk.

Household contracting and establishment of the Wenzhou model both benefited from the contributions of think-tanks, but the latter's biggest contribution was not in designing these reforms, but in helping communication between local and central, which made the central decision-makers believe that many of their worries about the reforms that had first of all been initiated by the regions were unfounded, and that some of the major risks perceived by their opponents were in fact spurious.

3.2. Collective Learning and Path Selection: How the Dual-Track Price Reform Concept was Formed and Realized

3.2.1. *The riddle of the dual-track pricing system*

The dual-track price system was the most distinctive of any of China's major economic reforms. It may not seem hard to understand today, but as with any reform that seems *ex post facto* to be quite natural, profound truths are hidden in its unfolding. The major difference between it and household contracting or the Wenzhou private enterprise reforms was that it was not a breakthrough firstly achieved in a particular place directly under the pressure of spontaneous public opinion, but was conceived by a minority of intellectuals, and hence had a certain *a priori* nature. This not only implies that it had more long-term social consequences than a spontaneous popular reform like household contracting, but also that it had greater historical contingency. Had it been some other price reform concept rather than the dual-track system that was realized, would history have been very different? This may be the eternal riddle of the dual-track price system.

Who first conceived of the dual-track price system? This is not such an important question in theoretical terms. More crucial is the following:

- How could such a non-mainstream idea become China's mainstream reform strategy?
- Taking into account the overall extreme poverty of theoretical knowledge in China's economic community at the time, the World Bank took the initiative in recommending experts in the Eastern European reforms to China. Why didn't China simply follow the opinions of foreign experts whose theoretical and empirical knowledge was so much richer than the Chinese?
- China's young economists were weak fledglings at the time, who had just started to assimilate western economics theories. How could such unknown young people, rather than the older generation of scholars, have had such a significant impact on China's economic price reform strategy?
- Why was the dual-track system feasible in China? Did this strategy have any universal significance? If so, in what sense can it be applied to other economies? In what sense is it an option only compatible with China's culture and system?

- In the development of China's reforms, did it do more harm than good or vice versa?
- Did its theoretical innovations provide any important inspiration?

I cannot comprehensively, systematically answer these questions here of course, but merely offer the views of one who witnessed it all. My main purpose is not to recite a piece of history, but to share with readers the insights I gained through it. To this end, I conceal the names of some of the people concerned, hoping to focus the reader's attention on the issues, and also because I am unable to keep track of all the important historical facts and figures connected to the dual-track price system. This was one of China's most controversial reforms. Anyone claiming a share of the "glory" should also bear historical responsibility for the negative consequences. Certain individuals played irreplaceable roles in the formation of the dual-track system, without whom history may have been completely different. However, I know from my experience of taking part in the reform that the "invention" of the dual-track system was not as important a historical contribution as some people think. The achievements of China's reforms were not due to some clever inventors; there were a large number of disinterested heroes, including many who were unsung and indeed tragic.

The experience of this period of history changed many people's lives, including mine, and so inevitably brings my personal prejudices into play in analyzing its course. I will do my best to not undermine the objectivity of the article. In hindsight, I think that the positive impact of China's reform and development of the policy processes and political environment that enabled the dual-track system reform to be produced and realized, go far beyond the reform itself. The previous section analyzed the political macroenvironment; this section sets out to answer the following question: what kind of public policy process was it in the 1980s that rendered such seemingly incredible reform ideas conceivable and realizable?

3.2.2. *Sharing knowledge beyond divisions of social status*

The reform experience of the early 1980s that I felt most keenly were the sincere exchanges which we as relative unknowns had with the reform leadership. Today's young people may not be able to imagine, let alone understand, how such sincere exchanges across huge divisions of social status could occur. Social status divisions undoubtedly form one of the biggest obstacles to collective learning in all societies. The stronger a society's ability to overcome this gap, the stronger its collective learning capacity will grow. A serious challenge to modernizing huge societies like China or India is how to cross this divide to mobilize the collective wisdom of society. That China's modernization took the costly path of radicalism is very likely related to the difficulty the lower and upper social strata had in communicating with each other. Fei Xiaotong at least criticized the indifference of the traditional Chinese scholar-officials towards the lower strata, while Weber pointed out that a cultural advantage of Christian civilization is that it favors the elite caring about the suffering of the ordinary people.

The Cultural Revolution clearly narrowed social distances between Chinese people. "Sending down to the countryside" and "re-education" on such a large scale, together with everyone being more or less equally poor, made the gap smaller and communication easier between different social statuses in post-Cultural Revolution China. However, this does not explain why the then leaders showed "public spirit" in their communication behavior. I agree with a friend's explanation of this issue: for some older revolutionaries of the time, while they were now confused about what was genuine socialism, the feeling that "the world belongs to the public at large" was still there. Having been "beaten down", these people had returned to the political arena, where they injected this spirit into the public politics of the day.

Post-Cultural Revolution China was filled from top to bottom with a ravenous hunger for knowledge. This thirst for knowledge on the part of the young was relatively easy to understand, but the strong enthusiasm for learning among the Chinese leaders who were already of advanced age was rare. This spirit of seeking knowledge for the public good was to help the Nongfazu (Agricultural Development Group) gain a privilege, namely to be allowed to recruit staff from among university students. This decision was to have a major and far-reaching impact on the reform policy process.

Mr. S was a talent discovered by the Nongfazu. He was from the countryside, and for many years had pondered its major economy issues. While his professional training at Beijing University had little to do with economics, he was quite fascinated with economic theory and became the first young person to make headway using Western economics to analyze the rural economy. In China in the early 1980s, there were inherently very few people who could master Western price theory, even fewer of whom had any in-depth knowledge of China's rural economy. Fortunately, the Nongfazu, having chanced across Mr. S's economic studies and recognizing that he was a rare talent, used its privilege to recruit him, rapidly raising this young agricultural policy think-tank's level of knowledge and analysis.

Mr. S made many important contributions to China's reforms, and many of the Nongfazu's important policy proposals were directly inspired by him. Many leaders of the reform, particularly Du Runsheng, learned a lot of economics directly from him too. His contribution to the dual-track price system reform was as follows:

He was the first to break through the theoretical framework of the planned economy, revealing that the essence of the price system under planning was to support industrialization by distorting prices. He revealed in particular that the policy of low-cost procurement under the *tonggou tongxiao* system was essentially a tax in kind levied on the peasantry.

He was the first to use the difference between rural market prices and the government price to explain the peasants' productive behavior, and explain fluctuations of the major agricultural products.

He was the first to propose orienting the reform of *tonggou tongxiao* to collecting tax in cash form as an alternative to compulsory procurement. He proposed that the government should buy grain and other agricultural products at market prices. This was the first theoretical analysis and policy suggestion in China to separate issues of the price mechanism from those of income distribution, and was a milestone in the reform learning process. Before Mr. S proposed his reform ideas, the idea of the planned price had always been dominant, thus stultifying thinking about policy options.

Mr. S's analysis and policy suggestions were refreshing, but went unrecognized by the theory and policy circles of the time and were not even officially released. This, however, did not prevent the Nongfazu from passing his ideas and suggestions to the highest policymakers. Du Runsheng and Wan Li both listened to Mr. S's proposals and realized at once that his proposal to "turn procurement into taxation" touched on a fundamental policy issue. While recognizing that this reform might involve a number of economic and political interests and that there may be significant political risks, they nonetheless supported and encouraged the bold explorations by young people, and never threw cold water on them.

3.2.3. *Bold experiments brought direct dialogue between theoretical vision and reality*

Between 1982 and the end of 1983, although Mr. S's reform idea of "turning procurement into tax" had won acceptance within the Nongfazu, they were still not able to completely win over the policy and theory mainstream in agricultural economics. In order to break this impasse, the Nongfazu proposed to Du Runsheng, then in charge of rural policy research, that they wished to go to a locality to carry out a pilot study to test the feasibility of this reform concept. At that time, the household contracting reforms had achieved full success. The central leadership was aware of the importance of feeling out the next stage of reform. In the spring of 1984, Du Runsheng formally approved the request.

That the request for a pilot study was approved and implemented smoothly, was thanks to the political reform situation of an upsurge in reform, as well as the high degree of mutual trust and mutual support between the central and local reform leaders. Du Runsheng phoned the then first secretary of Hebei, Gao Yang, who immediately indicated his welcoming of young people like us engaging in reform experiments in Hebei. The Hebei provincial leader in charge of agriculture, Yang Zejiang, soon notified all the relevant government agencies concerned with grain production, purchase and sale, to cooperate fully with our experimental work. We youngsters from the Nongfazu in charge of the pilot site were lowly in occupation and status, but this did not prevent us from accessing reports from various departments, transferring all relevant information, and asking them to fit in with our experimental work.

The success of household contracting reform gave the political upper hand to local cadres who had supported the reforms, providing our pilot site with an extremely favorable environment. Recalling those years, there was a tacitly understood "superconductivity" between the central and local reform leaders.

Mr. S was the major designer of this reform, while I was responsible for the pilot group. Gaocheng County in the Shijiazhuang region and Ningjin County in the Xingtai region were chosen for carrying out the pilot. The program for Gaocheng was the more solid reform scenario: farmers would pay the difference between the market price and the procurement price of grain as a resource tax to the government, thus gaining free cultivation rights, while the county government would complete the original procurement targets by purchasing through the market. We called this design a program for a "price differential tax". The program for Ningjin was quite bold: it would achieve not only food and fuel price liberalization, but also marketization of the prices of the main means of agricultural production, namely fertilizers and diesel fuel. In other words, the Ningjin pilot was the first free price reform experiment since the founding of the new China.

The pilot reform had the full support of the local government. The pilot group made a calculation of all major market prices and the price differential taxes the peasants should pay, and designed mechanisms for revenue compensation following the advent of market pricing for the government agencies engaged in grain marketing, circulating the means of production, and producers of fertilizer.

The biggest problems facing the pilot were, firstly, how to ensure that after market pricing, the balance of interests of all parties could be kept basically unchanged. For example, the food sector might be unable to fulfill the government's procurement targets because farmers paid too little price differential tax and the market price for grain was too high, or it might lose money if it fulfilled the procurement targets. Of course, farmers should not be required to pay high taxes because they had been given freedom in what they cultivated; supply and marketing cooperatives should not deprive the financial subsidies given to peasants by the state because they were selling fertilizer and diesel at market prices, and so on. Another problem was the "partial liberalization trap". On this score, the pilot team designed a bold program: they issued "circulation certificates", limited to use within the locality and which were equivalent to a local currency, to reduce the impact that the problem of inter-locality transfers of revenue, brought by liberalization of prices in localized areas, would have on the trial.

Also, the test team carried out a variety of cost calculations and interest negotiations with finance and food bureaus, supply and marketing cooperatives, and chemical plants, without which it would have been impossible to determine the total amount of differential price tax, scenarios for distribution of revenue and the amount of circulation certificates to issue.

By the summer of 1984, a historic turning point was seen in China's grain markets, when the market prices of food were for the first time comprehensively lower than the government's average procurement price. This situational change overturned the basic assumption of the pilot reform, i.e., that the government procurement price would be below the market price. The pilot therefore could not be completed in accordance with the predetermined plan. However, the experience with the pilot was extremely valuable, making us realize that liberalizing prices would inevitably hugely affect the existing pattern of interests, and such consequences could be very dangerous.

3.2.4. *Opening up public space, expanding opportunities for social elites to participate in the reform*

At the time, I was not aware of the great significance that the experience gained through the Ningjin pilot project would have for price reform. Hence, had it not been for the Moganshan Conference of 1984, the valuable knowledge gained from the pilot reform of "turning procurement into tax" in Hebei may possibly have become simply one person's empirical knowledge, and would have had no impact on the progress of China's reform.

The 1984 Moganshan meeting was an important event in the history of reform in China. Like many important historical events, as later people have gradually come to recognize its importance, it has become increasingly controversial. This is because analytical perspectives of those coming later are different, and also because time has erased many things from the memories of those present at the time. Some details that may seem important to latecomers were not so for a majority of those present.

One such issue is the dispute over who was the first to propose the dual-track system reform. While I know I myself was the first at the Moganshan meeting to suggest it, over the years I have not gone out of my way to emphasize this point because I do not consider that I myself made the largest contribution to formation and implementation of the concept. My reasons are as follows:

The Moganshan meeting was a successful collective action of young intellectuals with the support of the older generation of reformers, and I was not the planner or main organizer. The main purpose was to expand the opportunities for young economists to take part in the reform and compete with older economists in making plans for reform. Although I made a few contributions to this process, there were many other unsung heroes, some of whom I do not know to this day. One of the planners whom I do know, Mr. Z, proposed that participants be selected on the basis of the quality of their papers and the meeting be organized on the principle of exchanging countermeasures, which fortunately was accepted. Without this innovation, with everyone expounding their own articles as in the past, the Moganshan meeting would have been long forgotten.

On my arrival I learned confidentially that the central leadership, encouraged by the success of the rural reforms, had decided to speed up urban economic reforms, but the planned prices were proving to be a stumbling block. The central policymakers were thus in urgent need of a viable program of price reform. If the Moganshan meeting could contribute one, it would be a huge success and improve future opportunities for younger scholars to participate in the reform.

This news came from young scholars working in the core decision-making of agencies, and without their mediation it would have been impossible to bring the Moganshan meeting to interact positively with senior decision-makers and fully mobilize the participants' teamwork and team spirit.

Since we all knew that the price reform strategy was the jewel in the reform crown, from the very beginning, debate on this strategy became the hot spot of the meeting in addition to the formal agenda. This in turn opened up a special listing discussion in the evenings, in which the school of thought favoring free prices overawed the others; but the planned price school, representing the mainstream thinking of the day, was far from weak and proposed a reform policy based on adjusting the planned price. The two factions were evenly matched and stuck to their guns. Prior to the meeting, I had not conceived of dual-track reform, and only when there was a deadlock between the "release faction" who advocated free prices and the "adjustment school" insisting on planned prices was I suddenly inspired by my experience in Hebei. So, in the panel I chaired, I put forward the suggestion that "since neither school is feasible, we have to move to a dual-track system." In other words, without the atmosphere of free discussion, I may not have been able to have the "dual track" idea. Moreover, without the idea of "changing procurement to tax" suggested by Mr. S, or the Hebei pilot reform, I could not have had this conception.

Although the "dual track" idea was first raised at the meeting by me, the main proponent was not me, but Mr. H, whose eloquence quickly won the support of the majority of those present. More importantly, Mr. H later convinced high-level policymakers on behalf of the meeting. It is very important that a new policy idea be able to convince policymakers. I had many opportunities to meet with high-level decision-makers and propose a number of innovative policies, but most of the recommendations failed to convince them. Many clever ways have been found in this world, but only those that have won the confidence and determination of policy-makers have really made history. Therefore, the contribution of those who can convince the policymakers to accept creative ideas is greater than of those who invent them.

Of course, the greatest contribution was made by those who decided to adopt the dual-track approach. It was they who bore the enormous personal political risks in giving young people an opportunity to take part in the reform, while also bearing the risks of the reform policy itself. The dual-track price system was not without risk, as Zhao Ziyang, then leader of the State Council, made very clear. However, when discussing whether or not to pursue it, he expressed the indomitable spirit of "If I do not go down to hell, who will" and resolutely decided to accept the young people's recommendations. Reformers from the older generation like Zhang Jingfu and Du Runsheng also played an irreplaceable role. Without this enlightened reform leadership, even the cleverest conceptualization would have been in vain.

In short, the formation and realization of the dual-track idea was an achievement gained by fully bringing into play the collective learning capacity of China's elites in the reform process in the early 1980s, and was the crystallization of their collective wisdom. To exaggerate the creativity of a minority, while failing to notice the decisive role played by collective learning capability in the policy process, does not fit the facts.

The Moganshan meeting fully reflected this truth: a growing, public space with public rationality is extremely important for raising the collective learning capacity of social elites. Why was it that a group of unknowns could suddenly have a significant positive impact on the course of history? Was it simply due to their talent?

The Moganshan meeting was not an isolated event, but an important part of the process of the constant expansion of the public space in the early 1980s. Prior to this, the resumption of the college entrance examination and graduate education, the expansion of freedom of the press and of publication, and the acceptance of autonomous think-tanks taking part in the policy process all paved the way and enabled the Moganshan meeting. The planners, organizers and participants there were all a social elite, nurtured and winnowed out by this process. The expansion of public space in the early 1980s provided comparatively equitable participation opportunities for the growth and selection of this young elite, who gained a valuable public spirit from this fairness. Without this public spirit, it would have been impossible to have the discussion process of the Moganshan meeting with its public rationality. Even if the dual-track system had been proposed, it is doubtful whether it could have become a reform consensus.

In January 1985, just months after the Moganshan meeting, the dual-track price system became official Chinese government policy. This unique price liberalization strategy, in large measure, shifted China's market-oriented reforms into a completely different reform path from those of the former Soviet Union and Eastern European socialist economies.

3.2.5. *China's Enlightenment: Improving communicative (contact) rationality is the only way to break the doom of backwardness*

Undoubtedly, the dual-track price system, and in particular the policy process that produced reform strategy, left an indelible imprint not only on China but also on the entire historical process of socialist economic restructuring, the impact of which is still deeply felt 20 years later. However, we still cannot fully understand many major issues raised by the policy process and the reform strategy itself. The quest to solve the riddle has in fact only just begun.

3.2.6. *Was the dual-track system reform adventitious?*

Undeniably, as a historic event, there is something adventitious about the Moganshan meeting. If it had been canceled by the parties concerned, or if for some reason I had not taken part, there would then have been no conception of the dual-track system. If after the meeting, Zhang Jingfu had not had time to listen to the reports, if Mr. H had failed to convince Zhang Jingfu, if Zhao Ziyang had not dared to bang the table, ... , could the dual-track system have become a fundamental strategy in China's price reform?

In my understanding, Zhao Ziyang had at that time been quite appreciative of another conception of reform, which was what some called the "quick-step" program. The basic idea was to bring planned prices close to the equilibrium point by many comparatively quick adjustments. The proposers of the quick-step idea argued that its attractiveness lay in the fact that central finance did not need to spend much money to compensate for the interests harmed by the price adjustments, and could correct price distortions quickly while maintaining central control. If the dual-track system had not been proposed, there was a very big possibility that the quick-step would have been adopted.

But the problem was, could it succeed? If implemented, what would be the consequences?

Inferring from the existing experience and theoretical knowledge, the quick-step program was likely to have two consequences, the first of which would be to place unbearable pressure on the central planning departments. Those agencies and enterprises who stood to gain after prices were adjusted would of course be happier, but because the micro-incentive problem had not been resolved, there would remain a question mark over whether their efficiency and output could improve and thereby boost central government revenue. Meanwhile, agencies and enterprises disadvantaged by the price adjustments would be sure to exert pressure on the center for compensation, and might eventually form a strong resistance against the reform.

Unlike the "dual track", the "quick-step" program did the greatest harm to rural industries. This was because, theoretically, rural industrial enterprises were not entitled to allocations of major means of production by the state, and were subject in reality to great discrimination, greatly limiting their development opportunities. The biggest beneficiaries of the "dual track" were thus in fact these rural industries, because following implementation of the reform, small rural enterprises could buy and sell the means of industrial production at small transaction costs. Since production brigade firms had tremendous advantages relative to state-owned enterprises in terms of their incentive mechanisms and labor costs, the dual-track system gave them a great development opportunity, which thus became an important background to the rise of township and village industry as an "emerging factor" in the mid-1980s.

This showed that there were major institutional reasons why the dual-track system could work in China, i.e., the dual urban and rural economic system, without which there may have been problems with the feasibility of the dual-track system. Conversely, due to the existence in China of a dual economic system, the reality of this system was likely to sooner or later lead China toward a "dual track" or even "multi-track" price system. In fact, prior to the dual-track system, not only did multiple prices for the same things objectively exist, they had even been introduced into pricing policy. Of these, the most influential was the policy of *chaogou jiajia* (over-quota procurement at raised prices) in agricultural goods procurement.

In late 1978, in order to overcome the situation of acute shortage of agricultural goods, the central decision-makers decided not only to increase the grain procurement purchase food by 20 percent, but to pay the peasants an extra 50 percent for sales of grain over the state quota. After the implementation of household contracting, this policy had a tremendous incentive effect, and China even went into grain surplus. A major reason that I could suggest the "dual track" idea and other people could immediately understand it, was because we all knew that grain procurement was already in fact operating under a dual-track system. In this sense, China was quite likely to have had a dual-track system even had there been no Moganshan meeting. Of course, deliberately using the dual track to promote market-oriented reform would have had a completely different effect on the reform process than from being forced to accept it as a reality.

3.2.7. *Was the dual-track system of any theoretical value?*

The World Bank, which had long been concerned about and supported China's economic reforms, soon heard about China's dual-track price system. They were shocked by the Chinese people's decision and strongly questioned it. In their view, to have two prices for the same goods went not only against theory, but against common sense. A World Bank's expert panel, with Eastern European economists forming the core, formally proposed to the Chinese authorities that dual-track prices should not be maintained for long, but should be merged as soon as possible. But in fact, China's price reform program which hastily merged prices in 1988 strongly stimulated inflation expectations, which was to be one of the major incentives for the setbacks to the reform in 1989.

From the late 1980s to the 1990s, due to the success of China's economic reforms and economic growth, some overseas mainstream economists made a positive evaluation of the dual-track system (Byrd, 1987, 1989, 1991; Sicular, 1988; Lau, Qian and Roland, 1997, 2000). The Chinese translation of Roland's *Transition and Economics* (2000) gave it the following overall assessment:

"The dual-track system was an innovative institution in China's transition, characterized by being both efficiency-raising and Pareto-improving. The principle applies to other reforms and other countries: labor market reform, pension reform, and so on.

To some extent, most attractive about it was that, by preserving the rents of those hurt by the reforms, it made reform of the damage possible.

At the same time, the Pareto-improving feature of the reform did not mean that improving efficiency was at the expense of other goals." (p. 148)

Joseph Stiglitz, a Nobel prizewinner in economics and former chief economist and vice president of the World Bank, has reportedly described the dual-track system for the transition from planned to market pricing as a Chinese-discovered "solution of genius". Of course, having overseas mainstream economics scholars praise the dual-track system will not end the academic controversy about it, but it will drive scholars at home and abroad to take the academic investigation to deeper levels. The following is a list of a number of major academic problems triggered by the dual-track system:

1. Under what conditions does the dual-track system for product prices enhance efficiency, and under what conditions does it not?
2. Under what conditions is it Pareto-improving, and under what conditions is it not?
3. Given that the system is efficiency-enhancing and Pareto-improving, how are we to analyze the problem, noted by Roland (2000) from the Chinese experience, that it still faces real problems of moral evaluation and political constraint? Will simultaneous efficiency enhancement and Pareto improvement confer full legitimacy and feasibility on the dual-track system?
4. Directly related to issue no. 3, what relations are there between the dual-track system and corruption?
5. As a strategy for liberalizing prices in the transition from a planned economy to a market economy, what is the role of the dual-track system in the development of factor markets? Is it neutral or non-conducive to them?
6. Could a dual-track strategy also be used to promote the development of factor markets?
7. Could the consistent strengthening of modern values in China and developing countries be hindered by "generalizing" the dual-track reform strategy, thus locking them into a "disadvantageous" path?

Many of these issues, which are clearly of high policy and academic value, were induced from the practice of the dual-track system and raised for the first time by Chinese scholars. When we gathered in Moganshan 23 years ago to debate the dual-track system, quite a few people were not even clear what a factor market was. Chinese economists are now able to raise and analyze some of the most cutting-edge theoretical issues. The tremendous role that over 20 years of reform and opening up has played in promoting the cognitive ability of China's elite is a fact that speaks for itself.

A number of monographs could emerge from analyzing the above seven issues. This present essay can only review and comment on some of the points related to these issues, giving a broad overview of the topic.

Fairly rigorous analyses of the first and second of the above issues have already been made by economists; Roland (2000), for example, has given a very good overview in his monograph on the economics of transition.

Non-economists may note the following common-sense conclusion: the dual-track price system does not necessarily increase efficiency or achieve Pareto improvement. If the government continues to devote a lot of resources to expanding production of the planned segment, the overall efficiency improvement is questionable; at the same time, if it cannot enforce the planned (fixed) prices effectively, Pareto improvement may not be achieved. One of Roland's most important analytical results is that if there is no secondary market for the exchange of quotas for input goods, which means inefficient producers are allowed to re-contract their supply quotas to efficient producers at market prices, receivers of planned supplies may be more willing to sell their right to receive supplies to buyers who can pay more, compromising the dual-track system's efficiency increase (*op. cit.*, p. 143). Clearly, the existence of a large number of township enterprises in China provided ideal conditions for the formation of secondary markets.

3.2.8. *Dual-track pricing and exchange of entitlements*

On the third and fourth issues, that is, the relationship between the dual-track system and corruption, critics of the system accuse it of increasing the opportunities for corruption. Its defenders say that it is effective in breaking down the administrative stratum's resistance to economic reform. Both are correct, in my view. Critics of the dual-track system readily take the moral high ground, but their weakness is their inability to propose attractive alternatives. Their moral superiority is gradually undermined by the fact that their increased discursive power to criticize the dual-track system benefits greatly precisely from that very system.

It was through this critique that the concept of "rent-seeking" was introduced into China from abroad, becoming the most popular buzzword not only in economics but in popular parlance as well. I have been much enlightened by Barzel's (2002) criticism of the concept of rent-seeking in *A Theory of the State*. He argues that as an economic concept, rent-seeking damages the logical self-consistency of modern economic theory, which is based on the assumption of individual rationality. As a concept for describing amoral self-interested behavior, rent-seeking may be conducive to ethical critique, but not to economic analysis. So, what kind of economic self-interested behavior is not rent-seeking? Assuming that any rational economic system is based on the self-serving tendency of individuals, why should rent-seeking be separated from self-serving behavior, dividing the latter into good and bad? What difference would there then be between economic and moral analysis?

A major issue involving economics with the concept of rent-seeking is the exchange of the rent-sharing rights. But, far from helping us analyze this, it introduces moral criticism into rigorous economic analysis through the back door. Of course, such criticism against the rent-seeking concept is also no substitute for theoretical breakthrough on the exchange of rights. In the process of reflecting on the dual-track system, I gradually formed some new knowledge and concepts on the exchange of rights, which deepened my understanding of the theory of the dual-track system.

As Sen long ago noted, people have two kinds of entitlements: market entitlements and social entitlements. He argued that these two different types of entitlement or rent-sharing rights constitute a complete system of entitlements, and that there are profound ties between this system and poverty, and especially between the two kinds of entitlement (Sen, 1981). It is interesting that, in building his own theory of the state, Barzel also distinguishes between economic and legal rights. Sen's market entitlements and Barzel's economic rights are in my view quite similar. Both set out to describe rent-sharing rights that can be freely exchanged between individuals in a market economy. Barzel points out more clearly the direct relationship between economic rights and personal endowments or human capital, while the common feature between Sen's non-market or social entitlement and Barzel's legal rights is that they cannot be freely exchanged between individuals, because they derive from public power or from the "group domain", unlike market entitlements or economic rights which essentially derive from the "self domain".

This can therefore be summed up as human society having two different rent-sharing rights, one being entitlements in the "domain of the self", that is, rent-sharing rights based on private rights (the private exchange of which is, by nature, highly legitimate), while the other rent-sharing rights are entitlements in the "group domain", based on public power (the private exchange of which tends to lack legitimacy). However, as Sen and Barzel agree, there are important connections between these two rent-sharing rights: "group-domain entitlements" may effectively restrain "self-domain entitlements", and may have a profound impact on the economic behavior and level of welfare of society as a whole.

What, then, are the relations between self- and group-domain entitlements and the dual-track system we have been describing? The latter, I would argue, essentially involves the exchangeability of rights, in particular between self- and group-domain entitlements. The exchangeability of rights includes two factors: firstly, the legitimacy of the exchange in legal terms, and secondly, its technical feasibility; these two factors combined constitute exchangeability of the rights in question.

Superficially, the issue of concern for the dual-track price system is the problem of the right of free exchange of products, but this is essentially the problem of exchangeability of self-domain rights — without free prices of products, there will be no individual property rights; in particular, there can be no individual rights of free exchange of human capital rent claim rights. Under the planned economy, applying public power to carry out mandatory product prices and rationing seriously constrains each individual's economic freedom, thereby limiting the development of innovation and division of labor. Therefore, the two-track system marginally liberates free prices and expands the space for the exchange of self-domain entitlements, thus helping improve economic efficiency.

Most people have no difficulty understanding that free exchanges should be liberalized marginally rather than fully, because there is great uncertainty and risk if prices are suddenly liberalized fully. Criticism of the dual-track system focuses on the issue of corruption, which is actually the issue of fairness brought about by doubts as to the legitimacy of the exchange of the public and private rights due to the dual-track price system. This involves the issue of exchangeability between self- and group-domain entitlements.

Using public authority to serve private interest (which is an exchange between public and private rights) is indeed in conflict with modern concepts of social justice, but it cannot be denied that there are in reality cultural and institutional differences in how different societies define the boundary between the domains of the self and the group, and thus in the exchangeability of self- and group-domain entitlements. In China, development of the rule of law was suppressed over the long-term by a tradition of governance that saw the empire as a single household and family assets as the core of property rights, with the result that the boundary between the self and group domains was historically far less clear in China than in modern Western culture. A clear cultural characteristic of Chinese people is to accentuate distinctions between senior and junior and eminent and humble, whilst blurring those between public and private and group and self. It is an undeniable fact in the minds of Chinese people, therefore, that the exchangeability of self- and group-domain entitlements is relatively acceptable.

In addition to cultural factors, there were important institutional factors behind the ability of the dual-track system to work in China. When it was launched in the mid-1980s, genuine private enterprises in China were few in number and low in legitimacy. Trade in rent-sharing rights based on trading "quotas of under-priced materials" (what Roland (2000) calls secondary markets) occurred mainly between different "units" rather than between the public sector and individuals. Even when there were such transactions, individuals had to wear a "red hat" to gain legitimacy. In other words, the institutional factor of China's "*danwei* society" enhanced the legitimacy of trading power for money. I described China's property rights arrangement some years ago as a hierarchized collective property rights arrangement. Units with higher status have greater rent-sharing rights but little autonomy and low efficiency, whereas those with lower status have lesser rent-sharing rights but greater autonomy and hence more efficiency. It is precisely between units of different status that the bulk of the trade in rent-sharing rights related to trading "quotas of under-priced materials" is carried out.

Why was it that employees of relatively large SOEs with relatively greater rent-sharing rights in the planned economy most strongly opposed the two-track system, rather than collective enterprises and peasants with lesser such rights? Was there any rational basis for their fear and anger towards the dual-track system? The latter greatly enhanced the legitimacy of trading rent-sharing rights through production, inevitably putting pressure on inefficient producers to get out of production. The "dual-track system" did not, however, address the question of the exit mechanism of SOEs. In the planned economy era, employees of SOEs were provided with social security via their production rights being guaranteed by the state. The competitive pressure brought about by the development of the dual-track system threatened the production rights of the low-efficiency producers, thereby threatening the SOE employees' access to employment protection rights.

The concept of the entitlement system enables us to see that the basic characteristic of the entitlement system of the mandatory planned economy is to bundle the self- and group-domain entitlements together to restrict the exchange of rights, rather than as in a market economy's entitlement system where all rent-sharing rights, whether they be production-based or asset-based, are separated from social rights that receive basic safeguards, giving the economy great capacity for adjustment. Following the implementation of the dual-track system, we younger scholars who advocated the dual-track system, relying on instinct, devoted our research attention to reconstructing the microeconomic foundation and turning to the question of property rights, while its opponents either neglected or consciously avoided these core problems for a long time. This distinction is interesting.

Our concern with issues of micro-incentive mechanisms and property rights made us aware that the merging of pricing tracks was premised on improving the microeconomic foundations; but this idea faced a double obstacle politically. Those leaders who preferred to retain more elements of the planned economy argued that our ideas would in fact shake the foundations of the planned economy, while those hoping to accelerate market-oriented reform argued that our ideas were too long-term to solve the immediate requirements. Unfortunately, cognitive differences regarding reform in leading circles at that time displayed personal and politicized tendencies, adversely affecting rational discussion and choice of policy. It was against this background that speeding up two-track price mergers to curb corruption gradually gained high-level attention. This idea, at least on the surface, met the two political demands of accelerating the market-oriented reforms while evading the issue of property rights, as well as occupying the moral high ground by stressing fairness. A typical slogan of those advocating this was "control the money supply, decontrol the prices". Twenty years later, the absurdity of this slogan in the China of that time is apparent to all, but at that time, when China's theoretical circles were so limited in their knowledge of the market economy, once some Western mainstream economic idea seized the moral high ground, it could gain a level of discursive power in the policy discussion in China that is hard to imagine.

Following the political turmoil of 1989, a period of serious economic recession occurred in China and during this depression, the two-track prices of many materials merged. Corruption, however, far from disappearing, found greener pastures. While this helped to show that the dual-track pricing system was not the real source of corruption, this brought no end to the controversy over it.

3.2.9. The challenge to China's reforms of the "new dual-track system"

In 2004, 20 years after the dual-track system was proposed, harsh criticism of it appeared once again. This criticism, however, came not from its original opponents (though they by now controlled mainstream discourse), but from a new generation of economists; nor was their critical target the "old", but the so-called "new" dual-track system.

In the 1990s, while the forces that had once advocated it lost discursive control, the dual-track system became mainstream policy thinking, applying to almost all economic sectors such as factor markets, social security, housing, public services, and so on. This was the so-called "new dual-track system".

Zhong Wei, a critic of the "new" system, pointed out: "Beware of the 'new dual-track system'! It parasitically seizes on the great interests between the price system for commodities that is already marketized, and the price for factors that is as yet non-marketized. It is a bottom-up and continually self-reinforcing process, which, the more it uses opportunities for reform in capital, land, labor and state-owned enterprises, the greater its proceeds from corruption, and the more those who are involved in the game are excited and bloated. Too far removed from reform to ever 'merge tracks' with it, it is a vulgarized distortion of gradual reform because, to a large extent, what needs to be reformed are those who promoted reform years ago and whose vested interests under the 'new dual-track system' are still more than those who reject deepened reform. If we can say that the 'old dual-track system' was a progressive and partial innovation of the old system, the 'new dual-track system' is a regressive and comprehensive degeneration of the system. The crisis that has caused the current macroeconomic adjustment is exactly rooted in the great distortion of factor prices. Now, before we try to establish an orderly and normal factor market, we must first of all work on bottom-up grassroots democracy and on up-down construction of constitutional institutions."

Zhong Wei's criticisms are related to issues nos. 5, 6 and 7. As was the case with the critics of the "old dual-track system", the issues detected by Zhong Wei are all genuine ones; he expressed the disappointment and anxiety that many felt that the path of reform was diverging further away from the people's interests. But would his prescription be just like "manage the currency, liberate prices", too influenced by extraneous ideas and popular sentiment, and hence be extremely risky?

China's 30-odd years of reform have taught many a valuable lesson. A major one is that one should not be satisfied with criticizing the moral and political status quo, and not rush to offer prescriptions from the moral high ground. The existence of the "new dual-track system", or what Qin Hui calls the "dual-track syndrome", is really a great challenge to China's reform. But this is a challenge not only to those in power, but also to the whole of the Chinese elite as well; not only to their political leadership and moral steadfastness, but also to their collective cognitive capacities.

Criticism of the current state of China's "pan-double track" implies a major assumption, namely that the reform, having missed some important opportunities, has since embarked on a mistaken path, leading to today's less-than-ideal situation. That being the case, critics of the current state of affairs need to answer when exactly in the reform and what kind of opportunities were missed? Why were they able to be missed? What new means of cognition and theoretical tools would help us seize new opportunities?

Reflecting theoretically on these questions using the concept of entitlement, we have gained some interesting results. As noted previously, the basic feature of the socialist entitlement system is the bundling together of the entitlements of the self- and group-domains, restricting the freedom of exchange of rights by bundling these two with specific rights to production and occupation of assets, which is conducive to mandatory allocation rather than to market exchange. The "old dual-track system" separated the bundled-up entitlements only incompletely. The old dual-track system induced an exchange market in "quotas of input materials" such that self-domain entitlements (human capital rights) and group-domain entitlements (social security rights) were no longer bundled together with specific rent-sharing rights through production; however, the old dual-track system was unable to fully separate market and social entitlements bundled with their rent rights to occupy specific assets under the command economy, thereby constraining the development of factor markets. One of the most typical examples was that peasants' social entitlements must be bundled with their rights to agricultural land, regardless of whether they cultivated it or not.

As early as the 1980s, a series of spontaneous reform impulses took place in China's local governments, including privatization of industrial firms, grant of leave without pay, buying out residual terms of service, sale of urban *hukou*, etc., the essence of which was to dissolve (by means of exchange of entitlements) the bundling of asset-type rent sharing with human capital and social security entitlements. However, the mainstream thinking of the time could not accept the legitimacy of such entitlement exchanges. In the 1990s, the emergence of more forms of exchange of entitlements, in particular of social entitlements, made us aware of the possibility of developing social entitlement markets between local governments or group-domain entitlement markets. The legal and political issues involved in social entitlement markets were of course at that time much more complicated than markets of quotas for industrial materials, but such transactions which had already taken place in reality, as had happened with the exchange of commodity quotas, gave us a strong indication that this was an area very worthy of exploration.

If local governments were granted more autonomy (assuming overall control by the central government), and allowing the localities to adjust the size of government employees through buying out, trading quotas of new urban *hukou* and quotas for converting farm land for urban development, i.e., raise the tradability of quotas closely related to social entitlements (just like using exchange of "quotas for fixed-priced materials" to promote commodity markets), this would help achieve the goal of promoting the development of factor markets.

Interpreting evolutionary change in terms of the exchange of entitlements, we can understand the essence of gradual reform as constantly transforming the system of entitlements by exchanging them, of which how to design the exchange of old for new entitlements is the key to success in gradual reform.

Of course, the exchange of entitlements is not the only angle for reflecting theoretically on reform. In fact, reflection should be pursued on various perspectives like the process of politics, of policy, of moral collective experience, of psychological and cultural evolution, and so on, in order to really translate the history of reform into wealth for people in future. The most important perspective for theoretical reflection on the reform process is to view reform as a collective cognitive process.

3.3. Enhancing Communicative Rationality Between the Elite is the Only Way to Get Rid of the "Disadvantages of Latecomers in Development"

The greatest advantage of reflecting on reform from the perspective of collective learning is that it is conducive to transcending political and moral criticism to reflect on the process of policy reform. One of the most precious historical legacies that Deng Xiaoping left us with was that, in promoting reform, he wisely restrained from the bad tendency to excessively moralize and politicize cognitive differences over reform policy. This was an immeasurable contribution to upgrading collective cognitive capability among China's elite. Only by understanding "emancipation of the mind" from this perspective can Deng's political wisdom be really understood.

So why was it that, under the same "emancipation of the mind" slogan of Deng Xiaoping's, the course of the policy from the early to mid-1980s was very successful, whereas that of the late 1980s gave rise to big problems, until in the 1990s, the reform policy process was to run into more and more doubt?

The answer is simple. In the mid-1980s, communicative rationality significantly declined among the elite. What is communicative rationality? Habermas (1985) has studied this in great depth. The three criteria of rational communication he proposes are: truth-seeking, right-seeking and sincerity (three claims of valid communicative rationality: truth, rightness and sincerity [sic]). It is not difficult to understand communicative rationality in common-sense terms; put simply, rational communication is communication and interaction which seeks consensus rather than winning.

Looking at the interaction between China's elite from this point of view, it is not difficult to see that in the early 1980s, a great part of the communication between China's elite was consensus-seeking rather than winning, whereas this kind of communication would later become less and less prominent, and more and more difficult. The tragedy of 1989 was, to a large extent, the result of a failure of communication among the Chinese elite.

The significance of communicative rationality for humanity's collective learning is quite obvious. Human society is never free of conflicts of interest; people cannot but strive to come out on top, and if disputes over interests are all that is left in a society, interaction between people is only to define who wins. Thus, this society would be plunged into a "collective irrationality trap", consumed with irrational in-fighting. Enhancing communicative rationality can mobilize the collective wisdom of mankind, reduce unnecessary conflicts and achieve a better balance between competition and cooperation.

The complexity of the problem lies in the fact that humans seek, in the end, to come out on top. In order to increase the probability of doing so, they have to cooperate to raise their collective cognitive capability; but the latter is not determined by communicative rationality alone. Communicative rationality determines one, but not all, of the core elements of collective cognitive capability. As a result, in inter-group competition, at least in the short-term, a group with high communicative rationality will not necessarily be able to overcome one whose communicative rationality is low.

North (2005) points out that two other important factors determine collective cognitive capability: one is value rationality or the belief system, and the other the stock of knowledge. Although neither of these two factors is completely independent of communicative rationality, neither can be entirely generated from the interaction of a single group. As a result, a group whose internal communication has a high degree of rationality may well be defeated due to its inferior value rationality or stock of knowledge. What should the twists and turns of China's civilization in the process of modernization be attributed to? What has our civilization been doing wrong? This has for years been a lingering problem for China's intellectuals. Is it an institutional or a cultural problem? Is it a problem of the quality of the elite, or of the population's deep-rooted bad habits? I tend to think the biggest problem is one of collective cognitive capability. Of the three elements of collective cognitive ability, the biggest problem for Chinese people is the sphere of communicative rationality.

Over the long history of Chinese civilization, economic and social development has for a long time held the dominant position. The core values and stock of knowledge must have a certain amount of support, without which the achievements of ancient Chinese civilization would be incomprehensible. Why, however, is it impossible for China, like Japan, to successfully modernize its traditional values and knowledge at small social cost?

China's political system and political culture must bear some blame, but this general conclusion is not only unable to solve the problem, it may create more confusion. The trouble with both institutional and cultural determinism is that neither explains how institutions or cultures are selected by a society, and hence cannot answer the question of how to reform unsatisfactory institutions or cultures.

There is a tradition, deep-rooted in China's political culture, of either compromising to avoid a debacle, or scrapping everything and starting again. A major idea Barzel (2002) proposed in his state theory is that all state institutional arrangements in fact contain a mechanism of collective action to restrain state power. In China's imperial grand unity, state power was restrained by two mechanisms: one was the *daotong* ("moral authority") built on the scholar-officials' privileged explication of the classics, which could constrain the emperor's *zhitong* ("governance"); while the other was to make use of a peasant uprising to change the regime. The legitimacy of the latter mechanism was in fact implicit in the former — as soon as "orthodoxy" becomes a spent force, it becomes right and proper to rebel. In China with a powerful monarchy, the mechanism of *daotong*/orthodoxy is not reliable and has a tendency to constantly weaken, with the result that with the degradation and decline of gentry power, together with increasing external pressure, scrapping everything and starting again became more and more legitimate in China's political culture, reaching a peak in modern times.

The twists and turns of China's modernization show that its political culture is most deleterious to the communicative rationality of its elite, and a direct consequence of the elite's lack of communicative rationality is a huge social cost for China's modernization. It is not difficult to test the level of communicative rationality of the elite of a society in the process of modernization: it is clear just by looking at how much of the society's historical heritage of universal human values has been preserved in the process of modernization, and how much was destroyed in unnecessary conflict.

The deep link between communicative rationality and the relative success of dual-track pricing in the 1980s lies in the fact that the "old dual-track system" was the result of communicative rationality fully mobilizing the stock of knowledge, including making use of opportunities such as the old system of "trading quotas". The reason the "new dual-track system" was denounced was because the policy process leading to it was quite unlike that of the "old dual-track system", which mobilized the stock of knowledge of more people and more resources of the old system to serve reform. Although China's intellectual elite mastered more modern theories than in the 1980s, they lost many precious opportunities for reform.

What is the relationship between communicative rationality and political institutions and culture? Why is communicative rationality of special importance to the collective cognitive capability of developing countries in today's globalization? I conclude this article with a discussion of these two issues.

Political institutions and culture, in the environment of human communications, do indeed influence, but are by no means necessary conditions for, the probability of communicative rationality taking place and being successful. Rational political institutions and political culture are products of humanity's communicative rationality, and not the contrary. Otherwise, a state with political institutions and culture that are not conducive to communicative rationality would never be able to turn itself around. What, then, are the necessary and sufficient conditions for communicative rationality?

From a historical perspective, the threat or competitive pressure formed by an external environment with a plural power structure plays a very direct role in improving communicative rationality within the group. Such environmental pressures help force groups to form a pluralistic value perspective internally, and to form rational communication ethics and rules.

In today's highly globalized world, the pressure of external values and knowledge is immense. In this situation, a nation's capacity for collective self-examination of its own culture — above all, its political culture — becomes an important condition determining communicative rationality. The more a nation historically lacks a diversified power structure and a tradition of pluralistic values, the more difficult is its collective self-examination — this is the major challenge faced by modern China. However, having paid a great price, China has begun to mature in its cultural self-reflection. In recent years, Chinese intellectuals are again finding a balance between Lu Xun and Hu Shi, which is an encouraging sign.

In conditions where institutional and cultural support is lacking, the success of rational communication among the elite is significantly influenced by contingent, including political and technical, factors. The emergence of such political leaders as Deng Xiaoping and of information technology like the Internet has had a positive impact on communicative rationality. Reducing the political risk of communication is what they have in common. The fundamental reason authoritarian regimes rarely win against democratic systems is that in the latter, the political risks of communication are relatively low, so they can mobilize the wisdom of more people. As a result, the speed of China's democratization is largely determined by whether it can consciously innovate to keep reducing the risk of political communication.

Yang Xiaokai, an outstanding Chinese economist of the new generation, raised an important idea prior to his death: developing countries do not necessarily enjoy an "advantage" and may well suffer a "latecomer's disadvantage". In other words, it is hard for backward states to cast off the passivity of always keeping up the rear. Yang passed away before he could fully explain the mechanism of the "latecomer's disadvantage", leaving the problem for us.

It is not baseless paranoia, however. An important mechanism in its formation is that developed states can maintain their long-term comparative advantage in "communicative rationality", thereby keeping their innovative edge. Backward states, however, because they can reap the profits of new technology, lack the motivation to mobilize internal innovation and therefore lack either the motivation or ability to improve communication within their societies.

The mechanism of "latecomer's disadvantage" may have a direct bearing on the discursive advantage of developed countries. The advantage of developed states over backward ones in expressive or discursive terms constitutes a double-edged sword that is difficult to deal with. Thanks to the long-term advantages of their political systems and political cultures, developed countries not only possess long-term advantages in terms of the efficiency of their knowledge production — they also possess powerful discursive advantages in their moral, political cognitive and cultural expression. Advocates of the "latecomer's advantage" notice that backward countries can complete the technological progress already completed by developed countries in a shorter time, but they overlook something Yang Xiaokai noticed: in backward countries, technological progress can be independent of progress in political institutions or culture, and thus they remain backward in the long-term. Why does such a situation arise? Why aren't the backward countries forced to change their political backwardness by the overall advantage of the developed countries? One answer is that, when faced with the full advantage of the developed countries, backward country elites are forced to learn their discourses to be able to communicate with them; but in the process, many people lose interest and ability in communicating with those at the bottom of their own society and become an obstacle to its communicative rationality. A host of examples support this premise. The most prominent is the fact that many people from backward countries, having gained academic distinctions or a systematic education in developed countries, are given too strong a voice in their own country's political, policy and academic evaluation processes. While inevitable and playing an immensely progressive role, the collateral damage is very far-reaching as well.

A serious negative consequence is a lack of timely, effective communication and expression on major issues and knowledge that depend on local experience, and hence, missed opportunities for innovation and change. What is even more worrying is that the intellectual elite in developing countries steadily lose interest in addressing the intellectual challenge of their own countries' problems, devoting themselves instead to issues that are of concern in the developed countries, because only by contributing to addressing the latter's hot issues can they gain social recognition that gives them a voice in their own country. This can hardly fail to seriously distort political and policy processes in their homeland.

In recent years, I have been able to take part in two meetings of the Association of US-trained Chinese Economists, established by Yang Xiaokai himself and held annually in China. Two aspects left a deep impression on me. First, as soon as they had finished their keynote speeches, the bigwigs bearing high official rank and the aura of "returnees" left, utterly uninterested in listening to the little guys. Second, more and more young scholars go overseas to study social sciences without any local experience; many people are concerned solely with the technical details of various models, and have no qualms about using a Procrustean approach to study Chinese issues. One overseas student was working on urbanization in Shenzhen using only statistics for *hukou* rather than for the resident population, her foreign instructors no doubt unaware that 90 percent of the resident population in Shenzhen have no local *hukou*. What surprised me even more was that, with no foreigners present, even in the discussion of the so-called Chinese economic problems, many groups adhered to communicating in English and no one thought it unusual.

I do not know what Yang Xiaokai would have thought, but as a participant in the Moganshan meetings, I only know that if that year's conference had been organized by "returnees", with all communications in English, coming up with something like the dual-track system would have been quite out of the question.

The course of China's reform, as typified by the dual-track price system reform, provided an important lesson for other developing countries, namely that learning from developed countries need not be at the expense of communicative rationality in one's own society. While not easy to do, it can in fact be done. This has been borne out both positively and negatively by China's reform experiences.

Each country's path of modernization is different, and there is no one option. Modernization must undoubtedly avail itself of the values and knowledge resources of the developed countries, but if the values and knowledge resources favorable to modernization of one's own country cannot be mobilized, it will be easy to fall into a high-risk and high-cost reform path. The key knowledge that all countries need to reduce the costs and risks of modernization can only come from their own experience. The greatest challenge facing developing countries in shedding their fated backwardness, therefore, is their ability to fully mobilize foreign values and cognitive resources to make full use of local experience and wisdom. The core idea expressed in this article is that to cope with this challenge successfully, there is no alternative but to enhance our society's communicative rationality.

References

Barzel, Yoram (2002). *A Theory of the State: Economic Rights, Legal Rights, and the Scope of State*. Cambridge University Press.

Byrd, William A.:
———— (1987). "The Impact of the Two-Tier Plan/Market System in Chinese Industry," *Journal of Comparative Economics*, 11(3): 295–308.
———— (1989). "Plan and Market in the Chinese Economy: A Simple General Equilibrium Model," *Journal of Comparative Economics*, 13(2): 177–204.
———— (1991). *The Market Mechanism and Economic Reforms in China.* Armonk, NY: Sharpe.
Du, Runsheng (2007). "The Course of China's Rural Reform". IFPRI Occasional Paper.
Habermas, J. (1985). *The Theory of Communicative Action: Reason and the Rationalization of Society*, Vol. 1 (trans. Thomas McCarthy). Boston: Beacon Press.
Lau, Lawrence J., Yingyi Qian and Gerard Roland:
———— (1997). "Pareto-Improving Economic Reforms through Dual-Track Liberalization," *Econ. Letters*, 55(August): 258–292.
———— (2000). "Reform without Losers: An Interpretation of China's Dual-Track Approach to Transition," *Journal of Political Economy*, 108(1): 120–143.
Luo, Xiaopeng:
———— (1994). *Dengji Chanquan yu Gaige* (Hierarchical Property Rights and China's Reforms). Dangdai Zhongguo Yanjiu (Modern China Studies).
———— (2007). "Fuquan Jiaoyi yu Diqujian Xietiao Fazhan" (Entitlement Exchange and Balanced Regional Development), with Zhang, Xiaobo. Ershiyi Shiji Luntan (21st Century Forum), Vol. 99, February, Hong Kong Chinese University.
North, Douglass C. (2005). *Understanding the Process of Economic Change.* Princeton University Press.
Roland, Gerard (2000). *Transition and Economics.* MIT Press.
Sen, Amartya (1981). *Poverty and Famines: An Essay on Entitlement and Deprivation.* Oxford: Oxford University Press.
Sicular, Terry (1988). "Plan and Market in China's Agricultural Commerce," *Journal of Political Economy*, 96(2): 283–307.
Zhong, Wei (2004). "Return of New Dual-Track System: A New Burden to Chinese Reform" (Xin Shuangguizhi Fuzhi: Zhongguo Gaige Buneng Chengshou zhi Zhong?). First published in http://www.yannan.cn. Now available at http://www.usc.cuhk.edu.hk/wk_wzdetails.asp?id=3772.

CHAPTER 4

THE FORMATION AND EVOLUTION OF CHINA'S MIGRANT LABOR POLICY

*Cai Fang**

A policy adopted by governments in almost all developing countries is to provide the resource accumulation needed for industrialization by separating urban and rural factor markets, ensuring a higher standard of living for urban residents by making access to agricultural and rural resources unequal (Knight and Song, 1999; Anderson, 1995). While the planned economy era in China was no exception to this, it displayed at least two unique features. First, it was unique in separating urban and rural labor markets by means of a formal institutional arrangement — the household registration or *hukou* system. Second, the process of formation, improvement, and gradual reform of this labor market segmentation is

* Cai Fang is Professor and Director of Institute of Population and Labor Economics, Chinese Academy of Social Sciences, member of Standing Committee of National People's Congress of China, Vice Chairman of Chinese Association of Population, and member of 50 Chinese Economists Forum. He is a leading labor economist in China and has been deeply involved in labor market reforms over the years. His major publications include *The China Miracle: Development Strategy and Economic Reform* (Hong Kong: Chinese University Press, 2003, coauthored). Under the planned economic era, farmers had to live and work at their place of birth under the strict *Hukou* system. Labor mobility was largely prohibited. After three decades of reform, China boasts the largest scale of internal migration in the world, although the *Hukou* system has not been fully eliminated yet. The massive shift of labor from the low-productivity agricultural sector to high-productivity industrial and service sectors greatly contributes to China's rapid economic growth. In this chapter, Dr. Cai narrates the formation and evolution of China's migrant labor policy over the past several decades.

now virtually complete. These reforms may thus constitute a good example of institutional change.

The economic reforms which began in China in the late 1970s, and the growth effects they have delivered, have been accepted around the world and have aroused high levels of interest in other countries, especially developing countries with similar institutional starting points. Reform of China's labor mobility policy has not in fact, as some scholars (e.g., Lardy, 1994, pp. 8–14) assert, lagged behind the progress and extent of other areas of reform; it has, as an important component of economic reform, stayed in overall touch with its rhythm and mode and shares the typical features of China's reforms. A review of the formation and reform process of China's labor mobility policy, analyzing the political economic logic it followed, may be instructive for scholars and policymakers in other countries.

4.1. The Logic of Formation of the Household Registration System

After the establishment of the PRC in 1949, the Chinese Communist Party (CCP) began promoting industrialization, and in the 1st Five-Year Plan period (1953–1957) established a development strategy which prioritized heavy industry. To develop heavy industry under scarce endowment of capital resources, it was necessary to lower input costs, including those of labor and food. The government therefore monopolized the circulation of agricultural products, carrying out a policy of purchase and sale at low prices. In this policy of *tonggou tongxiao* (monopoly purchase and sale), to prevent loss of production factors in agriculture it also carried out collectivization of agricultural production, forming the People's Communes, and further restricted the mobility of the most active factor of production — labor — through the household registration system. *Tonggou tongxiao*, the People's Communes and the *hukou* thus constituted a "troika" in the institutional arrangement of China's agricultural economy in the planned economy period.

Initially, the household registration system did not set out to prevent movement of population, but simply to register it. The *Constitution of the PRC* promulgated in 1954 provided that "citizens have freedom of movement and residence". Until the first half of 1956, government documents regarding household registration required no mandatory restrictions on migration or labor mobility. Eventually, however, a series of conditions were to turn this institution into a component of the planned economy dividing the urban from the rural labor market. These conditions lay primarily in conjunction with the two other parts of the structural "troika", together with institutional arrangements linking it to other components of the planned economy.

In 1952, land reform was completed nationally, giving land to the peasants. They were, however, to lose direct ownership of their land again when mandatory collectivization commenced in 1956. By 1958, 99.1 percent of peasants participated in People's Communes, in which land was collectively owned. Starting in 1956, the drawbacks of collectivization were demonstrated in the form of agricultural failures and famine, due in particular to the implementation of the *tonggou tongxiao* policy; the peasants' rights to food were deprived, and the first victims of food scarcity were those who had produced it. In Chinese history, a mass of landlessness and hunger is usually accompanied by the formation of displaced persons. In the late 1950s, peasants went to the cities in search of jobs, hoping to join in the bustling economic construction of the time and share the fruits of economic growth.

However, on the one hand, under the development strategy of giving priority to heavy industry, industrialization did not provide enough jobs for workers moving out of agriculture, while on the other, migration and labor mobility came into conflict with the exclusivity of urban employment and social security. Spontaneous labor movement was eventually prohibited by policy, and the peasants' right of "exit" was curtailed. Rural migrant labor was excluded from both the urban-rationed grain supply which formed in the 1950s, and the urban employment and social security based on employing units. From late 1956, moreover, the central government announced a series of regulations to suppress the flow of the rural workforce. With the "PRC Ordinance on Household Registration" of 1958, a household registration system was officially formed that divided city from country, and impeded migration and the flow of labor. The system was to continue up to the eve of reform in the late 1970s.

The household registration system that China implemented in the planned economy period differed from those in other countries in that its purpose was to fix distribution of population and allocation of labor between city and country. According to the regulations, a person's household registration was enacted after birth, according to the location of the mother's household registration. Unless the government thought there were sound reasons, or it accorded with the unified arrangements of economic planning, no one could change his or her registration in their lifetime. Specifically, regional transfer of population was controlled by quotas of public security agencies, and rural-urban migration was virtually impossible apart from that arranged by plan. Movement of labor between industries took place according to the deployment plans of departments of labor or personnel, and no spontaneous labor markets existed.

4.2. Household Contracting Liberates Workers

The formative history and logic of the household registration system show that its substantive content was not only to restrict household registration — its core was to restrict transfers of population and of the sectoral employment of agricultural labor, to exclude the rural population from urban welfare systems, and exclude rural workers from possible jobs in non-agricultural industries. W. Arthur Lewis would later show that a dual economic structure existed in developing countries, formed under conditions similar to the divided labor market that the registration system and related institutions had led to in China. On the one hand, the expansion of the "price scissors" between agricultural and industrial products caused an income gap between urban and rural areas; on the other hand, the household registration system also led to urban and rural residents having unequal access to the fruits of industrialization. At the same time, it led to tremendous losses of efficiency in resource allocation.

The agricultural economy under this dual structure was seriously inefficient. Regarding how agriculture should be organized, Mao Zedong said in 1958 that the advantage of People's Communes was that they unified industry, agriculture, commerce, science, and the military, which helped leadership. Specifically, the organizational structure finally chosen for People's Communes was "three levels of ownership based on the production brigade". This form of organization merged all the factors of production in the countryside, restricting activities to a defined area with no freedom of movement. For rural workers, there was neither the right to leave a People's Commune, nor freedom of movement beyond it, thus greatly damaging the incentive mechanisms of their work.

Characteristic of collective work in a production team was a lot of empty sloganizing and eating out of one big pot: the work points earned by each worker were fixed, so that the distribution (of rations and cash) at year's end was carried out by the production brigade according to the number of days' labor each worker had recorded. The production resulting from doing more work would be shared equally by all the team members, and the burden of losses due to laziness would be shouldered by all. Hence, half-hearted effort was an inherent malady in the People's Communes, leading to declining agricultural production efficiency.

The food requirements of the cities and industry were, however, absolutely guaranteed. The result was a long-term failure to improve rural income levels and standards of living. Having built up somewhat over a certain period, this situation would give rise to strong resistance to the existing institutional arrangements underlying the low efficiency. As a way of withdrawing from the commune, the workers, lacking any right to leave, would work even more half-heartedly. In addition, the cultivation of agricultural products was in strict accordance with the provisions of the plan. To guarantee the food supply, production was structured in accordance with the principle of "grain as the key link". The great majority of the rural labor force was concentrated in cultivation and not allowed to engage in industry of business, so peasants' incomes were very low. 250 million rural residents were in a state of absolute poverty nationwide in 1978, and the income gap between urban and rural areas reached 1:2.57 (setting the per capita income of peasants at 1). At that time, given the necessary political conditions, a fundamental system change was bound to happen.

At the time of the Third Plenum of the 11th CCP held in Beijing (winter 1978), 18 peasants in Xiaogang, a village in Fengyang County, Anhui, went against general opinion to become the first to engage in household contracting. All problems of food and clothing were at once solved, and the effect spread like wildfire. After this, encouraged by gradual relaxation of government policy, the household contract system rapidly spread nationwide. In early 1980, only 1.1 percent of production brigades were practising the household contract system, reaching 20 percent by the end of that year. The figure was 100 percent by the end of 1984, and 97.9 percent of peasants were by then practising it.

The specific method of the family contract system was to give back the land originally under the collective unified management of the production team to the peasant household, according to its head-count and working strength. Having finalized its agricultural tax and procurement obligations, and paying deductions to the collective, the household would keep the remaining product, i.e., have claim to any surplus over and above what they themselves had put in. This operational mode, while not legally changing the collective nature of land ownership, greatly stimulated labor incentives, and production was greatly enhanced immediately. According to scholars, about 46.9 percent of agricultural output between 1978 and 1984 can be attributed to the national inception of this change (Lin, 1992).

With this manifold increase of the work effort, there was a significant decline in the labor time needed for agriculture, and a labor surplus emerged. To absorb it, peasant households, which now had operational autonomy, firstly switched their work from being used solely for grain production to other agricultural sectors, and then from cultivation to the overall development of agriculture, forestry, animal husbandry, fisheries and household sideline production, greatly changing the agricultural production structure and improving labor utilization and income levels.

While most observers highly praised the family contract system for improving the effectiveness of work incentives, after the increase in production efficiency, this system had a more important effect on the peasants' reallocation of labor — namely, by engaging their enthusiasm and granting them autonomy in arranging the time, method and content of their work, the peasants' labor was liberated. Therefore, this reform can be viewed as the point of departure and basis for the reform of worker migration policy.

4.3. From "Leaving the Land But Not the Hometown" to the "Tide of Migrant Workers"

With the improvement of agricultural productivity, the capacity of either cultivation or "big agriculture" (including forestry, animal husbandry, sideline production and fisheries) to absorb labor was ultimately limited. However, in the early 1980s, the government did not encourage labor to leave the countryside. Noting the necessity of transferring agricultural labor, and the development potential for small rural industries located in the countryside, the government promoted a mode of agricultural labor transfer of "leaving the land but not the hometown", i.e., encouraging peasants to shift out of agricultural production to employment in township and village enterprises (TVEs). Professor Fei Xiaotong, a Chinese sociologist with high official status, captured this in theoretical terms as an economic development model with Chinese characteristics (Song, 2006).

The labor force employed in brigade enterprises numbered 28.27 million in 1978, rising sharply to 69.79 million in 1985. In 1987 Deng Xiaoping said, in praise of the TVEs, that "he himself had never anticipated this result". However, in 1985, the 370 million rural people who had transferred to jobs in TVEs accounted for only 18.8 percent, and some 300 million workers remained in agriculture. According to the prevailing estimates, about 30–40 percent of the agricultural workforce — in absolute terms, about 100 million to 150 million — was surplus (Taylor, 1993, Chapter 8).

Faced with the surplus labor seeking jobs, the government expanded the policy of "leaving the land but not the hometown" to encourage farmers to shift to small towns. Professor Fei Xiaotong provided a theoretical basis for this policy, which he expressed as "small towns, big problems". While at the time small towns saw great progress, towns of this size, due to their lack of jobs, were in the final analysis limited to being destinations for transferring around 100 million surplus rural workers. Given that reform in the cities, particularly in the state-owned enterprises, had yet to get underway, rapid development of the TVEs was due to use of the pressing demand for consumer goods when people's income levels had increased, availability of capital goods and the implementation of the two-track system in the markets for products and production materials. With the acceleration of urban reforms in the mid-1980s, the development of TVEs began to falter. Peasants thus began to transfer to large, medium and small cities in search of non-agricultural jobs.

The gradual removal of various institutional barriers was crucial to the transregional flow of workers. Since the 1980s, the government gradually lifted the policy of restricting the mobility of rural labor. In 1983, with channels for transfer *in situ* of the rural labor force becoming narrower, the government began to allow peasants to engage in long-distance transportation and sale of agricultural products, legitimizing remote operation for peasants for the first time. Controls on labor mobility were further relaxed in 1984, and workers were even encouraged to take jobs in nearby small towns. By 1988 the central government set a precedent when it allowed peasants, prior to abolition of the grain coupon system, to bring food supplies into the cities, to take jobs and set up businesses.

In the 1990s, the central government and local governments took a series of measures to relax policies restricting migration, implying a certain degree of reform in the household registration system as well. For example, many cities of all sizes had long implemented the "blue *hukou*" system, which allowed buying a quasi-urban status for cash and changed the absolute restriction of household registration into selective acceptance. This was progress of a kind. Moreover, in 1998 the Ministry of Public Security gave a green light to the number of people entering the cities. If children could carry out household registration with either parent, couples who had long been separated could get together and obtain a change of household registration; the elderly could obtain city *hukou* along with their children, and so on. Although resistance to these reforms was encountered in some major cities, further reform of the household registration system was at least provided with a legitimate basis at the central government level.

By the 21st century, the decision-making power for timely reform of the household registration system was actually devolved to local, in particular urban, governments, forming three models of reform.

The *first model* was typified by reform of the household registration system in small towns, characterized by "minimum conditions and comprehensive liberalization". In 2001 the State Council approved and circulated the views of the Ministry of Public Security on promoting reform of the household registration management system for small towns, and from October 1 of that year, reform of this system went from pilot mode to full implementation. In more than 20,000 small towns nation-wide, the basic condition for registration was reduced to just "having stable sources of life and legal domicile in the city"; any outside overseas individuals or families meeting these conditions could apply to obtain an urban *hukou*. This can be said to represent the largest reform step taken since the *hukou* system was implemented in 1958 — a quite thorough reform of the household registration system.

Typified by medium-sized cities and provincial capitals, the *second model* was characterized by "abolish quotas, grant conditional access". As comprehensive reform of the household registration system for small towns was pushed ahead, many medium-sized cities and even some provincial capitals made major efforts to reform their household registra-tion systems. Their approach was to relax the eligibility criteria, substantially lowering the threshold for settling in the city. For example, a condition for Shijiazhuang (capital of Hebei) was "holding a city labor contract for two years and above". This model was adopted by some medium-sized coastal cities with relatively rapidly developing markets and lively economies, and large and medium-sized cities in the central and western regions eager to quicken the pace of development. Reforming the household registration system in this way was consistent with the objec-tive requirements of fostering the labor market, but also with the gradual mode of promoting reform.

The *third model* was typified by Beijing, Shanghai and other major cities, and was characterized by "building a high threshold and opening city gates". While many small and medium cities were relaxing their household registration restrictions, Beijing, Shanghai and other major cities gave a green light for the introduction of special skills only, while on the other hand raising the entry thresholds for ordinary workers. For example, Shanghai even halted the implementation of the blue *hukou* sys-tem whose thresholds were high to begin with. The result of raising the threshold would hence not lead to an opening of the city gates. Comparatively speaking, reform of the household registration system in these cities made no substantive progress.

In reality, institutional factors restricting the flow of labor were not lim-ited to just the household registration system. Urban welfare reform creates an institutional environment for the flow of rural workers to the cities. The urban economic reforms that gradually came into force in China in the late 1980s, such as the great demand for workers created by the development of the non-state-owned economy, reforms of the food rationing, housing distribution, healthcare and employment systems, have all reduced the costs to peasants of moving to the cities, settling down and finding work.

As the outcome of a series of institutional changes and policy adjustments, the scale of rural labor mobility has grown, forming the "dearth of migrant workers" which has caught the attention of the world. There has never been a consistent official figure regarding the migration of rural workers, and scholars often roughly estimate on the basis of partial surveys. In what follows, using an induction that has been made before, we give a broad account based on numerical changes in inter-township labor mobility prior to 2000 (Ministry of Agriculture Task Force, 2001). As estimated by the State Council Development Research Center (a Chinese government think-tank), in 1983 there were only 2 million rural migrant workers, increasing to 30 million by 1989; and according to a Ministry of Agriculture estimate, this reached 62 million in 1993 and 75.5 million in 2000. By 2000, the National Bureau of Statistics annual survey had estimated the figures shown in Table 4.1.

Table 4.1. Numbers of Migrant Workers and Its Ratio to Urban Employed (Unit: 10,000 people, %).

Year	Migrant Workers	Urban Employed	Ratio
2000	7,849	21,274	36.9
2001	8,399	23,940	35.1
2002	10,470	24,780	42.3
2003	11,390	25,639	44.4
2004	11,823	26,476	44.7
2005	12,578	27,331	46.0
2006	13,212	28,310	46.7

Sources: "The number of migrant workers" from the National Bureau of Statistics; Rural Socioeconomic Survey Corps (Rural Division), China Rural; *Household Survey Yearbook* (various years), China Statistics Press. "Urban Employed" is from the Division of Population and Employment Statistics, National Bureau of Statistics, and the Planning and Finance Division, Ministry of Labor and Social Security, *China Labor Statistics Yearbook* (various years), China Statistics Press.

4.4. From "Paradox of Numbers" to "Law of Supply and Demand"

The rural-to-urban transfer of labor was no triumphant forward march running completely smoothly. In positive terms, the central government initiated "leaving the land but not the hometown" in the hope that surplus rural workers would stay in the TVEs. In negative terms, in the early 1980s, the central government still frequently issued documents stressing the need to strictly curb recruitment from the countryside, even calling for cutting and reversing rural employment programs. In the mid-1980s, central government policy began changing from strict prohibition to control of the tempo. At the same time, many local governments in the very long-term followed the thinking of the planned economy era, which saw the migrant workers as a "blind flow", a blindly floating population. Urban residents often held an unwelcoming attitude toward them. One foreign scholar even asked with some feeling, "Why does the China media always report negatively on the floating population?" (Davin, 2000).

When examining the relationship between the urban employment situation and attitudes towards the floating population, my collaborators and I found that whenever employment pressure, or the overt or covert unemployment rate rises in the cities, city governments are inclined to take a more stringent policy toward the floating population, adopting an attitude of exclusion towards outside labor (Cai *et al.*, 2001). Clearly, urban residents and governments regard the outside labor flow as competitors for employment.

When the urban residents' concerns about external labor taking their jobs are aggravated, they are usually expressed in some way. At the same time, reforms create a dual character in the part of the media: on the one hand, they are required to stay consistent with the government's principles, intentions and main concerns, while on the other hand they have to survive in a competitive market, and thus to a certain extent speak for the local residents. This double bind or dual objective reaches a consensus in attitudes toward the mobile population. In other words, if urban people form exclusory sentiments *vis-à-vis* the floating population due to being threatened by concerns about their jobs, the media is happy to express this for them, because it is often a concern of the local government.

Passing through specific political channels, the voice of local residents and the media, thereby affects local policy measures regarding the mobile population. Under the existing system, local governments are usually evaluated by a set of performance appraisal mechanisms. There is usually a series of indicators for assessing local governments, some of which are rigid, known as the "veto system". "Occurrence of major group incidents" is one such rigid indicator, i.e., if it is ever substandard on this score, whatever the government may have achieved on other fronts will be offset in the examination results. Large-scale unemployment is a ready instigator of group incidents.

On the other hand, the performance of local government is also evaluated by the results of People's Congress elections. In the existing People's Congress system, ward-level deputies are directly elected by residents with local household registration, and the ward-level People's Congress in turn elects city-level deputies. The Municipal People's Congress approves mayoral and deputy mayoral appointments and audits the city government's work report, thereby directly or indirectly evaluating the government's performance. Although the voices of the people cannot be expressed directly, they can also affect the behavior of the government indirectly through the local media. The external population remain eligible to vote in their hometowns and not in the destination, hence their voices are never fully reflected in the cities.

More importantly, given the dual economy which still relies on the countryside to provide resource accumulation for industrialization, the policy trend of the entire urban-rural relationship is still dominated by the renowned "paradox of numbers": while the peasants are many in number, their residence is scattered, their cost of collective action is high, and their negotiation status in policy decisions is low (Olson, 1985). In contrast, while the urban residents are small in number, they are concentrated in political centers both great and small, where their collective action readily affects social stability; hence, their wishes are of greater concern to policymakers. Over a very long time, urban attitudes to migrant workers are therefore unfriendly. These attitudes are strengthened or weakened according to the state of urban employment, and the institutional basis of this differential treatment is the residence registration system. In other words, although the process of reform enabled rural workers to cross regional boundaries to work and reside in the cities, migrant workers and the floating population are subjected to unequal treatment in urban areas.

Above all, they are excluded from jobs. Whenever there is pressure on jobs, many cities, in order to protect local urban workers' jobs, often announce and implement manifestly discriminatory employment policies, e.g., that the only jobs open to the floating population are those that local workers are unwilling to do. External workers thus can work only in the self-employed and informal sectors, or with non-formal employment status in the formal sector. In extreme cases, city governments take measures to drive the migrant population out.

The second major issue is wage discrimination. Investigations have shown that in cities, the average wage of migrant workers is only 70 percent that of the local workforce. Of this wage gap, some 43 percent cannot be explained by differences in level of education, but is caused mainly by the factor of discrimination with regard to household registration status. In addition, foreign workers are excluded from both the physical welfare and housing incentives that local businesses provide for their workers.

Third is exclusion from social security and public services. Minimum-standard living program and unemployment insurance, which are now universal in cities, are directed solely at local residents, and the migrant population is not covered. Policy requires the extension of equal treatment (including guaranteed age care and medical insurance) to migrant workers, but the coverage they receive is actually very low. In addition, the compulsory education migrant children should receive also faces problems of difficulty with admissions and high fees.

Solinger (1999) predicted that were the demand for labor for urban development to increase substantially and/or more job security established for urban workers, fundamental changes might take place to the household registration system dividing urban and rural labor markets. As a matter of fact, not only are such conditions for change constantly accumulating, but a dramatic turning point was also reached in 2003.

Beginning in that year, a "dearth of migrant workers" appeared in the Pearl River Delta, and the supply of basic migrant labor was unable to meet enterprise needs. So far this phenomenon has not disappeared or been mitigated, but has in fact spread to other parts of the country, even to labor-exporting regions in the central and western provinces, and by 2007 there was a broad shortage of basic workers. Behind this phenomenon are changes in the population growth rate leading to a decrease in the working-age population (in rural areas, this has decreased in absolute numbers). Therefore, it is not a short-term or cyclical phenomenon, which implies that the Lewis turning point in the course of economic development, characterized by the depletion of rural surplus labor, has been reached.

Direct observation of the distribution pattern of the rural labor force can confirm the judgment that the Lewis turning point is approaching. In 2005, of 485 million rural labor resources (according to conservative estimates), some 200 million underwent *in situ* or outward transfer to non-agricultural industries. Agriculture still needs a workforce of 178 million, but about half of the 100 million surplus labor force is already over 40 years of age (Figure 4.1). Once the pool of surplus rural labor is dry, it marks the beginning of a change in the dual economic structure. This does not mean that there is no potential for transfer of rural workers, but only that if there is no increase in wage levels or equivalent strengthening of other incentives, non-agricultural industries will no longer have easy

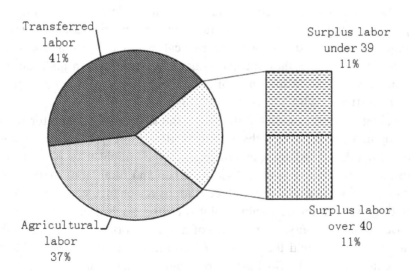

Fig. 4.1.   Distribution of rural workers (2005).

Source: Cai and Wang (2007).

access, as in the classic dual economic development period, to the labor supply they need.

Changes in the long-term relationship between supply and demand in the labor market lead to a corresponding shift in the mode of influence of different groups over policy, from the minority-dominated "paradox of numbers" to the "law of supply and demand", wherein the majority play a role (Olson, 1985; Anderson, 1995). A series of changes hence takes place in the equilibrium between interests, which affects the influence of different social strata on government policies and their relative bargaining position in institutional arrangements, which in turn may lead to an acceleration of reforms in migrant labor policy. In 2000, relevant central government documents began to display active support and encouragement of migration by the rural workforce, and clearly proposed reforming the institutional segmentation between city and country, eliminating the guiding ideas that unreasonably restricted peasants migrating to the cities for work. This was known as the unitary urban-rural employment policy.

The trend of this policy is unambiguous and stable, and in the years since has been increasingly stressed in relevant government documents, and was clearly written into the 10th and 11th Five-Year Plans published in 2001 and 2006, respectively. Moreover, by encouraging the flow of labor through the creation of fair conditions to improve the migrants' employment, accommodation, children's education, and social security, these policies have gradually became enforceable measures.

The "Sun Zhigang incident", which happened in coastal city Guangzhou in 2003, clearly symbolized a major change in policy orientation. A 27-year-old university graduate, Sun Zhigang, was employed in a garment company in Guangzhou, where, due to the lack of a local *hukou* or local temporary resident permit, he was detained by the police and beaten to death. This attracted widespread public criticism targeted directly at the unreasonable institutions behind the criminal acts of the law enforcement officers. When the perpetrators were brought to justice, strong criticism of the system of household registration and temporary residence permits was set off nationwide. The central government also attached great importance to this, evidently seeing the inconsistencies between the current system, the laws of economic development and the requirements for a harmonious society. Hence, only three months after the

"Sun Zhigang incident", the fastest adaptive reform of an institution that had been seen in history subsequently took place, namely the abolition by the State Council of the "Approaches to the Custody and Repatriation of Urban Vagrants and Beggars" which had been in force for over 20 years, together with the promulgation of "Approaches to Aiding and Managing Vagrants and Indigent Beggars", which fundamentally changed the orientation of policy for urban vagrants — from detention to aid — and abolished the institutional basis for law enforcement officers to intervene in population movement.

In 2006, Document No. 5 of the State Council entitled "State Council Suggestions on Solving Certain Issues Regarding Migrant Workers" upgraded the encouragement, guidance and help of the flow of rural labor to the level of "conforming to the objectives of industrialization and urbanization", focused attention on solving major problems in the interests of the rural migrant workers, and proposed the principle of "fair and non-discriminatory treatment". Passage of the *Labor Contract Law* in 2007 indicates the great importance that the government attaches to protection of the rights and interests of ordinary workers, including the migrant workers, and the policy orientation altered tremendously. In the same year, the "Employment Promotion Act" directly targeted barriers to employment faced by rural migrant workers, by providing that: "rural laborers going to work in the city enjoy equal labor rights with urban workers; setting discriminatory restrictions on rural workers going to work in the city is prohibited."

These policy changes are, in the final analysis, positive responses of the Chinese government to realistic institutional demands, and thus conform to the requirements of change in the course of economic development. They may therefore eventually find expression in genuine improvements in the conditions of migrant workers. Prior to 2003, the basic wage levels of migrant workers saw no change over recent decades, but with the emergence of the labor shortage, they increased by 2.8 percent in 2004, 6.5 percent in 2005, and 11.5 percent in 2006 (outstripping the growth rate of the economy). At the same time, due to the intervention of and role played by policy, migrant workers' wage arrears have decreased significantly, and their working and living conditions have improved.

4.5. Conclusion

I have stated elsewhere that an immense rural reform took place in 1978, when the income gap between rural and urban areas had reached 1:2.57, prompting China's peasants to unhesitatingly and comprehensively "exit" from the constraints of the People's Commune system. The moment the urban-rural income gap returns to those levels, a new institutional change will occur (Cai, 2007). In 2006, the income gap between urban and rural areas was exactly 1:2.57 (using constant 1978 prices). This is no coincidence. This time, China's peasants were "voting with their feet" by means of migrant labor. The ideal of building a harmonious society initiated by the Chinese government was consistent with the direction chosen by the peasants.

Therefore, not only have the migrants obtained a good environment such as they have never had before, but the government has also launched the strategic approach of New Rural Construction, taking as the next key steps the establishment of a unified urban and rural employment and reform security system. The urban-biased policies so widespread in developing countries, and of such deep concern to development economists, have begun to come to an end in China.

China's experience of reforming its migrant labor policy shows that successful reform is a process of balancing the benefits received by various interest groups. In the initial phase, making the majority of peasants who seek living essentials and wealth benefit quickly from the process of labor migration is a low-cost, high-yield political decision, whilst with the expansion of the group benefiting from it, the reform process deepens and strengthens itself. However, ready-made institutional arrangements assume a state of equilibrium. Attachment to the principle of gradual reform breaks this pre-existing equilibrium between institutions. One cannot expect to bring reform to completion in a one-time breakthrough. The thoroughness and forward tempo of reform does not depend on the size of the groups who directly benefit, but on their policy influence. The negotiating status they have can, in a non-steady-state demographic structure, change with changes in the population.

Lewis (1958) made a forecast of the time of arrival of the turning point for the Japanese economy on the basis of its demographic trends.

However, this does not imply passively waiting for natural conditions to mature.

The reform of China's migrant labor policy can be seen to be incomplete at each stage. But as a result of this process, on the one hand, the peasants directly benefited as a group by having their incomes increased; and on the other, they became an important source of China's economic growth (Cai and Wang, 1999). The reforms can thus be constantly deepened and advanced. As the demographic structure naturally changes — i.e., with the gradual decline of the rate of growth of the population of working age — the surplus rural labor force is gradually being completely absorbed; therefore, boosting incentives to promote labor mobility is becoming key to benefiting all inhabitants. The conditions for more thorough reform will then gradually develop.

References

Anderson, K. (1995). "Lobbying Incentives and the Pattern of Protection in Rich and Poor Countries," *Economic Development and Cultural Change*, Vol. 43, No. 2, pp. 401–423.

Cai, Fang (2007). "Rural-Urban Income Gap and Critical Point of Institutional Change," *Economic Change and Restructuring*, forthcoming.

Cai, Fang and Dewen Wang (1999). "Zhongguo Jingji Zengzhang, Kechixuxing yu Laodong Gongxian" (The Sustainability of China's Economic Growth and the Contribution of Labor), *Jingji Yanjiu* (Economic Studies), Issue No. 12.

Cai, Fang and Meiyan Wang (2007). "The Counterfactuals of Unlimited Surplus Labor in Rural China," *China and World Economy*, forthcoming.

Cai, Fang, Yang Du and Meiyan Wang (2001). "Huji Zhidu yu Laodongli Shichang Baohu" (*Hukou* System and the Labor Market Protection), *Jingji Yanjiu* (Economic Studies), Issue No. 12.

Davin, Delia (2000). "Migrants and the Media: Concerns about Rural Migration in the Chinese Press," in West, Loraine A. and Yaohui Zhao (eds.), *Rural Labor Flows in China*. University of California, Berkeley: Institute of East Asian Studies.

Knight, John and Lina Song (1999). *The Rural-Urban Divide, Economic Disparities and Interactions in China*. Oxford and New York: Oxford University Press.

Lardy, Nicholas R. (1994). *China in the World Economy*. Washington, D.C.: Institute for International Studies.

Lewis, Arthur (1958). "Unlimited Labor: Further Notes," *The Manchester School of Economics and Social Studies*, Vol. 26, No. 1, pp. 1–32.

Lin, Justin Yifu (1992). "Rural Reforms and Agricultural Growth in China," *American Economic Review*, Vol. 82, No. 1, pp. 34–51.

Ministry of Agriculture Task Force (2001). "Zhongguo Nongcun Renkou Bianhua he Tudi Zhidu Gange Yanjiu" (Demographic Change in Rural China and Reform of the Land System), topic report, Beijing.

Olson, Mancur (1985). "The Exploitation and Subsidization of Agriculture in the Developing and Developed Countries," paper presented to the 19th conference of International Association of Agricultural Economists, Malaga, Spain.

Solinger, Dorothy J. (1999). "Citizenship Issues in China's Internal Migration: Comparisons with Germany and Japan," *Political Science Quarterly*, Vol. 114, No. 3, pp. 455–478.

Song, Linfei (2006). "Zhongguo Jingji Fazhan Moshi de Lilun Tantao: Fei Xiaotong de Yixiang Zhongyao Xushu Gongxian" (Theoretical Account of China's Economic Development Model: An Important Contribution to Scholarship by Fei Xiaotong), *Jianghai Xuekan* (Jianghai Journal), Issue No. 1.

Taylor, J.R. (1993). "Rural Employment Trends and the Legacy of Surplus Labor, 1978–1989," in Kueh, Y.Y. and R.F. Ash (eds.), *Economic Trends in Chinese Agriculture: The Impact of Post-Mao Reforms*. New York: Oxford University Press.

CHAPTER 5

NARRATIVES OF WENZHOU'S INDUSTRIAL PRIVATIZATION

Zhu Kangdui*

5.1. Research Summary

During the reform era, Wenzhou was the district where marketization and privatization were implemented to the greatest degree. This, coupled with the pace of its economic growth and its level of prosperity, has generated much interest in the Wenzhou phenomenon.[1] Journalists and scholars, both within China and overseas, have drawn various lessons out of

---

* Zhu Kangdui is a professor at the Wenzhou Public Administration Institute. He has interviewed all the mayors and Party secretaries of Wenzhou City that have served since the late 1970s, and has written extensively on Wenzhou's economic reform. At the outset of the Chinese reform in the early 1980s, private ownership was largely taboo. Wenzhou City pioneered a series of institutional reforms to promote private sector industrial development, which were later adopted by the rest of China. This chapter details the process of Wenzhou's industrial reform. On one level, the Wenzhou reform and development model has emerged out of enterprising and innovative activities of private individuals struggling to break free of the poverty trap. On another level, it is also the result of the conscious decision of a local government, beholden to the conflicting pressures of central government policies and local realities, to take its lead from local realities and respect the innovative spirit of the people. The experience of Wenzhou shows that under the conditions of a strong state and strong ideological constraints, policies and reforms initiated at the level of local government can create a liberal environment for the local economy, and can also provide positive feedback for the process of economic reform on the national level.
[1] The disposable income of urban residents in Wenzhou City in 2006 was 21,716 yuan, ranking third in the country after Dongguan and Shenzhen.

Wenzhou's experience. Some scholars have explained it as the product of a local government strategy of "rule through non-action". Others have approached the issue from a different perspective to show that the Wenzhou model was "forced" or "liberated" into existence.

The *People's Daily* opined that, aside from these factors in the success of the Wenzhou model, "another very important factor is that the Wenzhou Party Committee and City Government have consistently given priority to practice over theory, and have had the courage to implement innovative policy measures."[2]

The economist Professor Zhang Wuchang, after conducting a field survey of Wenzhou in September 1987, said that one of the most important factors in explaining Wenzhou's economic success was the low preponderance of state-owned enterprises at the onset of reforms, and therefore a low degree of state monopoly control. This meant that there were many unutilized paths to development upon which the new ownership system could be implemented. In addition, looking from the perspective of the market, the Chinese domestic market in the early years of the reform had great potential, driven by a great private demand for consumer goods. From the time of their establishment, the enterprises of Wenzhou targeted their goods for sale in the national domestic market, and so had the lead on enterprises from other regions. This created a larger space for the regional economy to expand into.

Parris (1993) described the emergence of the Wenzhou model as the result of conflict, compromise and ongoing negotiations between local individuals, the local state and the central government bodies — a process in which local officials played the key role.

Liu (1992) believed the Wenzhou model to be the most famous model representative and typical of the regional pattern of modernization. The key to its success lay in "adapting traditional institutions to modern conditions". More specifically, the formula of its success can be reduced to the combination of "three M's" with "one I", i.e., Mass initiativeness, Mobility, and Markets, and the Interstices in the architecture of the Chinese economy. Liu strongly emphasized the importance of the pre-existing

---

[2] Liu Zhengui *et al.* (1986). "Realistic approach, creative practice: survey of family business development in Wenzhou", *People's Daily*, 7,8.

tradition of the Wenzhou regional economy in the emergence of the Wenzhou model. He described this regional tradition as historical local response to environmental and political pressures, and hence saw the Wenzhou economy in the reform era as the continuation of practices of emigration and long-distance trade through which Wenzhou people had responded to social and environmental pressures in the past. Therefore, Liu believed, from a practical perspective, that the Wenzhou model (being the model that "travelled the furthest" of all the development models of the Chinese socialist economy) was certainly driven by enterprises and agents of the private sector, but also by the versatile policies of local Party and government departments and the political support of grassroots organizations. Even more importantly, the Wenzhou model, during crucial stages of its development, received the enthusiastic support of pro-reform national leaders.

Du Runsheng, at a symposium convened to promote the lessons drawn from the experiences of Wenzhou and Taizhou (held on May 25, 2000), pointed out that Wenzhou's economy was privately orchestrated, privately operated, privately possessed and privately enjoyed; it was a self-generated and stable sustainable economic order. History teaches us that self-generated orders bring forth the practical example of a pioneer who draws in others, and are continuously improved through a process of mutual rivalry. The result is new institutions and a new economic system — this is the general pattern, and Wenzhou's economy is a practical demonstration.

The above analyses all reflect, from various angles, the reasons behind the emergence of the Wenzhou model. However, why was it that Wenzhou was able to walk this arduous and precipitous path of reform within the specific socio-economic and political constraints of the time? In particular, why was it Wenzhou alone that chose decisively to walk the path of privatization and marketization, when systemic factors differed little across all of China? And by what means did Wenzhou lower the input costs of reform and guard against political risks? In order to answer these questions, we must retrace our steps to explain, in addition to the general macroeconomic processes, the logic behind the proactive decisions made by private agents and the government in the specific historical context, using our knowledge of the historical evolution of the socio-economic system.

5.2. Research Approach and Analytical Framework

We may assume that the local government in Wenzhou, as with all local governments throughout China, is a rational person that seeks to maximize utility. In the process of making decisions to further the reforms, it must make up-to-date appraisals of the magnitude of costs, risks and returns of reforms based on all the relevant information available. Accordingly, it can make decisions to advance or retreat, in order to maximize the returns of reform and minimize the costs and risks.

Under the constraining conditions created by top-down supply of power, one of the important factors in local government achieving maximal utility with minimal cost and risk is that its reform choices are able to "hold up the heavens and stand firm on the ground". The former means that the reform measure conforms to the wishes of the central government or is at least within the permissible range of reform measures. The latter means that the reform measure is in harmony with the actual local context or, put another way, is able to secure the support of the local population.

Accordingly, top-down reforms require a relaxed hand to encourage popular support, while bottom-up reforms need to gain central government sanction. If these conditions are not fulfilled, top-down reforms that run contrary to the wishes of the masses will be subject to opposition and resistance from the masses, thus affecting the efficiency of their implementation; meanwhile, bottom-up reforms that fail to gain the support of the central government will always be subject to central government suppression and penalization, and so will be unlikely to be sustained. The attitude of different government levels to a reform measure is invariably determined by the assessment made by relevant leaders of the wishes of their superiors and the situation on the ground. This assessment is therefore grounded in the command at each government level of information from the central government and from the locality. Due to differences between the various levels, and the loss and misinterpretation of information through the process of transmission and reception, the information from different sources available at each level of government is asymmetrical. In general, higher levels of government will have access to more information on the wishes of the central government, while lower levels of government will possess more information on the real situation on the ground. Furthermore, as times and conditions change, the demand and will for reform at different central and local levels will also be subject to change.

The plurality, mutability and asymmetrical information in the will to reform at different levels of government is the cause of the complex trade-offs and differences of opinion found in relation to decisions pertaining to many key aspects of economic reform.

In the to-and-fro between central and local government, the transmission of the wishes of central government leaders is able to directly change the orientation of local government activities. At the same time, the trial measures implemented by local government are at times able to serve as excellent practical demonstration for the central government, and so further promote the reform process on a national level.

While investigating the grand wave of privatization and marketization in Wenzhou, I reviewed not only the published academic literature on Wenzhou, but also the corpus of local newspapers from Wenzhou published during the reform era. I also interviewed several hundred participants in the process, including the successive Party secretaries installed at the head of the Wenzhou City Government since the 1980s. My aim through this has been to gain insight into the reform process as experienced by decision-makers at the local level, and therefore gain an accurate feel for the internal logic of self-initiated reforms. In light of the fact that Party and Government in China are institutionally integrated, the use of the term "local government" in this chapter refers to the local government and Party executive collectively.

5.3. The Initial Conditions of the Self-Initiated Reforms in Wenzhou

To properly understand the full drama of privatization and marketization as it unfolded in Wenzhou, we cannot ignore the specific conditions that prevailed in Wenzhou prior to the beginning of the reform period.

Wenzhou is located in south-eastern coastal China, at the southern end of Zhejiang Province, and encompasses a land area of 11,784 sq. km. Historically, Wenzhou was a prosperous commercial city with a thriving handicrafts industry, and the transport and trading hub of southern Zhejiang and north-eastern Fujian. After the signing of the Treaty of Yantai in 1876, Wenzhou was forced into becoming an open port, and from this time foreign firms entered the district in force. Subsequently, during the war years, the local economy suffered substantial damage. When Wenzhou was liberated in 1949, the city precinct had only small-scale privately-owned enterprises, comprising 374 handicraft workshops that employed about 5,000 people, with fixed assets of 1.328 million yuan and industrial output valued at 64.23 million yuan in 1980 constant prices.

Due to Wenzhou's location on the coastal line of defense, the central government, out of strategic considerations, invested little in Wenzhou. Up until 1978, the central government had invested a combined total of 559 million yuan in the district, amounting to 88 yuan per capita, which was one-third of the province-wide average figure of 240 yuan per capita. With the further shock of the Cultural Revolution, the Wenzhou economy was on the verge of collapse. On the eve of the reform period, the population of Wenzhou was 5.61 million, but the arable area amounted to only 2.98 million *mu* or 0.53 *mu* (0.2 acres) per head, one-third of the national average, while the rural net income averaged 114 yuan. Of the 3,000 households residing in the Jinxiang township of Pingyang County, there were 3,579 people between the ages of 16 and 46 awaiting employment. These people repeatedly petitioned the township secretariat demanding food and work. The number of urban unemployed youth in Wenzhou City was as great as 45,000 people.

To break out of the cycle of poverty, prior to the reform period the Wenzhou local government repeatedly criticized aspects of top-down policies in the traditional system that did not conform to realities on the ground or the economic laws of production. Early in May 1956, the deputy secretary of Yongjia County, Li Yunhe, sent a team of cadres to the Liaoyuan Advanced Collective in Sanxi district to implement a trial program of household responsibility. Other villages followed this example. From early 1957, a total of more than 1,000 rural cooperatives in the Wenzhou district had implemented a household responsibility system, with a membership of 178,000 households, or 15 percent of collectivized households.

On January 27, 1957, *Zhejiang Daily* published an article by Li Yunhe titled "'Specialization' and 'Household Responsibility' are good methods in solving the central contradictions of the collectives". On October 31, 1957, *Xinhua News Agency* published an article entitled "Strengthen the enterprise of collectivization, abandon the capitalist road", criticizing the household responsibility system, and criticizing Li Yunhe by name four times. Subsequently, a number of cadres in Yongjia County were labelled as "rightists", while Li Yunhe was designated an "extreme rightist", expelled from the Party, stripped of all his duties and sent to a factory to perform manual labor. But this did not cleanse Wenzhou of its preference for the household responsibility system. After this incident, in rural Wenzhou, particularly in mountainous and semi-mountainous areas, clandestine implementation of the household responsibility system continued. In 1975 and 1976, the household responsibility system accounted for 77 percent of rural households in Yongjia County, while in mountainous areas the household contracting system covered one-third of households. In the winter of 1976, at the 2nd National Agricultural Conference to promote the spirit of the Dazhai Commune, Yongjia County was the county named as the "most serious case of sabotaging the collective economy by dividing the land and going it alone".

At the same time, the Wenzhou people attempted to find their own way to break free of the cycle of poverty. When rural youths completed their studies, many went on to learn a trade and became carpenters, painters, brick layers, shoe repairers, tailors or cotton winnowers. In the townships of Jinxiang, Qianku and Yishan, over half the labor force left their homes in search of work. It is said that those who left their homes to beg amounted to nearly one-third of the total population. Urban unemployed youth who were unable to find work registered their personal files under household enterprises and, under the pretence of being subsidiary factories, engaged in processing work.

Purchasing and sales agents of commune enterprises often did not take all of their business back to the commune, but secretly gave a portion of it over to private workshops. Aside from this, private involvement in goods trading continued unabated despite repeated attempts to ban such behavior. As reported in the *Wenzhou Gazetteer*, in 1970 there were 5,200 unlicensed goods traders in Wenzhou, which increased to 6,400 in

1974 and 11,115 in 1976. At the same time, there were a number of under-
ground construction teams and transport businesses, as well as a black
market in manufacturing resources. In 1976, four people from Wenzhou
including Chen Pingjiang, Qin Wenxiao and a Mr. Liao were sentenced to
death for engaging in speculative trading. But no matter how many times
the "tail of capitalism" was cut off, it always grew back. Clearly, in the
face of the restrictions enforced by the planned economy system,
Wenzhou people with their talent for non-capital-intensive business
operations were always able to eke out an existence between the cracks in
the old system.

To solve the survival dilemma faced by its people, local officials in
Wenzhou made great efforts to implement trial reforms of the old system.
In the name of this cause, some local officials were forced to pay a heavy
political price, while some local people were forced to pay with their
lives.

5.4. Initiative of Local Government and Society at Different Stages of the Reforms

In the face of the situation of supply shortages and poverty brought about
by the planned economy system, the second generation of leaders of the
Chinese Communist Party (CCP) made the decision to launch the reforms.
However, in the early reform period, even within the central leadership
there was no clear understanding of what exactly should be reformed, by
what means, and to what degree. There were also differences of opinion
on these matters. Accordingly, in the gradual reform approach represented
by the political slogan "cross the river by feeling the stones", each local
government made its own assessment of the intent of the central government and of local conditions and, based on this, made its own reform
choices, thereby developing different development models. The most
famous of these were the Pearl River Delta model founded on the
principle of drawing in foreign capital, the Southern Jiangsu model based
on developing township and village collective enterprises, and the
Wenzhou model characterized by private enterprise. Of these, the
Wenzhou model attracted the greatest amount of socialist critique, due to
its trademark feature of giving primacy to the private economy. This made

it the reform path of greatest cost and greatest political risk. If that was so, then how did the people and local government of Wenzhou come to choose this unsubsidized and politically risky path of reform?

5.4.1. *The courageous trials of the early reform period (1978–1985)*

In 1978, when Wenzhou received the news that the family contract system had been implemented in Xiaogang Village, Anhui Province, the process of redistributing the management of land from the collective to the household was initiated in many villages. After the release of central government Document No. 75 in 1980, the process of turning over all production to the household unfolded rapidly, and over 90 percent selected the more radical "household contract" system.[3]

The implementation of the household responsibility system quickly released surplus labor from the villages. As the number of Wenzhou locals looking for work outside their home district increased, they tended to be relatively quick in hearing news of shortfalls in the supply and demand of manufactured goods. So they decided to make use of their strength, and entered the long-distance redistribution market.[4] However, as there were severe shortfalls in domestic production capacity, with demand far outstripping domestic supply, some were able to make the most of lax central government policies to develop household industries engaged in small goods production, using traditional technologies and household labor and production space. This type of production required little investment, was quick to establish, employed simple technology and had few barriers to entry. Some of these enterprises began to engage in smuggling industrial goods across the national border. For example, in the area around Huanghua and Qiligang in Leqing County, and the area around Jiayuan Village in Hupulin, Pingyang County, relatively large-scale smuggling activities emerged between 1979 and 1980.

---

[3] According to the author, in 1985 on the outskirts of Beijing's rural survey, many suburban and rural areas of Beijing began household contracting only in 1983, and some did not have it until 1985.

[4] This was an unlawful act of profiteering.

The situation described above, combined with the factional legacy of the Cultural Revolution and contradictions caused by the coexistence of overlapping district and city administrative entities, left the provincial Party committee with the impression that Wenzhou was a rather chaotic place. In order to address this chaos, in August 1981 the provincial Party committee of Zhejiang Province appointed the provincial standing committee member Yuan Fanglie to run Wenzhou. After his arrival, he made lots of noise about solving the problem of leadership unity by merging the district and the city governments and implementing a tiered city-county administrative structure. At the same time, he led the country in waging a strike-hard campaign against crime and social disruption. In early 1982, the State Council and the Standing Committee of the National People's Congress issued a document titled *Notice on a strike-hard campaign against serious crimes in the economic sphere*. The provincial committee of Zhejiang also launched a strike-hard campaign against speculative trading and smuggling activities in the Wenzhou district. Out of this came the famous "incident of the eight grand kings" in Liu City.[5] In the wake of the campaigns, many people involved in different aspects of goods trading such as long-distance redistribution either went into hiding or fled the district, and the Wenzhou economy went into a tail spin (see Figure 5.1).

In September 1982, Yuan Fanglie participated in the 12th National Congress and was elected as a provisional member. Deng Xiaoping gave the opening address to the Congress, and Hu Yaobang presented the report *The new status of modern socialist development*. At this meeting, the central government demanded that the thrust of national policy be redirected towards modern socialist development, and also raised the target of "doubling twice". When Yuan Fanglie recalled how the 12th Congress had transformed his thinking, he said:

"As a delegate to the 12th Congress, I was able to personally listen to the delivery of the report. I thought that the most thirst-quenching, most encouraging aspect was the line by Deng Xiaoping that 'poverty is not

---

[5] The "Eight Grand Kings" incident referred to eight famous specialized households in Liu City, Yueqing County.

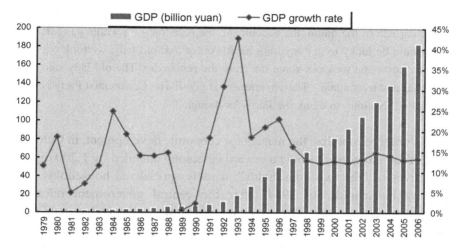

Fig. 5.1. Wenzhou's economic growth since reform.

socialism'. Why did this leave such a great impression on me? Because at the time it was said that in Pingyang County, a third of the population of the entire county were begging for their food. On learning this I thought to myself, 'Whatever the ideology behind it, when I have food I say to myself that whatever ideology fills my stomach is laudable. Begging is not socialism. If I say something wrong here, if someone wants to take me before a judge, I could say that this line was said by Deng Xiaoping. How impoverished had my Wenzhou become! A whole county of several hundred thousand people reduced to begging!'

When I returned to Wenzhou in search of a strategy to develop the economy, I led other members of the city leadership committee to investigate and ask questions in the streets and villages. In Tangxia township, I met an old lady who was engaged in the production of elastic. For an investment of 500 yuan of equipment, she was able to generate an annual income of 6,000 yuan. I did a sum in my head: the profit of one old lady equals 6,000 yuan. Of ten old ladies it would be 60,000 yuan, and of a hundred it would be 600,000 yuan — equivalent to a state-owned enterprise! Back then there weren't many state-owned enterprises with an annual profit greater than 600,000 yuan. Even if one did make a profit of 600,000 yuan, it would still have to distribute this between the head of the equipment factory, the branch secretary, the chairman of the union, the accountant, the registrar — a whole gang. It would be lucky to get anything back! As for that old lady, we took out her costs and took out some tax from the remainder. The old lady said over and over again, 'The government is good! The Communist Party is good!' Nothing to thank the Party for though."[6]

In order to mobilize the masses for economic development, in October 1982 Yuan Fanglie convened a reward ceremony attended by 1,200 representatives of "the two households", namely specialized households and priority households. In 1984, after the central government released Document No. 1, the Wenzhou city committee launched a publicity campaign around the rehabilitation of the "eight grand kings", announcing their release without a criminal offence. In the same year, several meetings directed at city and township industry were convened to loosen the fetters of industry. Yuan also succeeded in convincing the head of the Agricultural Bank to allow all of the local credit societies in Wenzhou to implement a reformed system of floating interest rates, and thereby solved the crucial issue of enterprise funding. With the support of local government leaders, on October 29, 1984, Fang Peilin of Qianku township in Cangnan County launched the first private bank (*qianzhuang*), Fangxing Money Lenders. To develop township and village industry, local governments even went so far as to appoint the owner of a private enterprise, Ye Wengui, as the vice-head of Jinxiang district in charge of industry. In 1984, the government of Longgang township in Cangnan County took the bold step of selling land use rights, which they did under the rubric of collecting an auxiliary services fee for public utilities. This resulted in the rise of the peasant-funded peasant city of Longgang. This measure of selling land use rights according to the quality ranking of the land broke from the long-standing practice of free auxiliary services according to the established plan for city land. Later, when the experience of Longgang was applied in the reconstruction of Wenzhou, the procedure followed relied on private funds, demonstrating the path to urbanization through the market methods of the Wenzhou model.

---

[6] My interview with Yuan Fanglie (oral material).

These bold reforms sent a message to the people that developing the private economy was permitted. The people's confidence in developing the private economy was greatly increased, and Wenzhou's urban and rural economy developed rapidly. For example, the total industrial output value of the downtown Lucheng district was 150 million yuan in 1984, of which the street enterprises accounted for 110 million yuan, a growth of 83.86 percent on the previous year. Profit grew by a total of 100.25 percent over the same period, thus doubling that year.[7]

Wenzhou's rapid economic development caught the attention of the central leadership. On November 28, 1985, Premier Zhao Ziyang went there. After his visit, he pointed out that Wenzhou could set up a pilot area. When Yuan Fanglie asked him what would be piloted, he replied: "You pilot how the people can get rich without costing the Center anything." However, while Zhao Ziyang, Wan Li, and others from the central leadership boldly supported it, interpretations of Wenzhou differed greatly within the central leadership. Some people agreed cautiously, while others strongly questioned or even resolutely opposed it. Wang Fang, then Provincial Party Secretary, wrote in his memoirs:

"In 1985, a group of old comrades in the Central Advisory Commission came to Hangzhou after visiting Wenzhou to exchange views with me. On the one hand, they affirmed that the Wenzhou practice was revitalizing the economy and people's living standards had been significantly improved; on the other hand, they were not unworried: was this in line with the socialist orientation? Would the consequences of this practice continue? At the time, leaders of more than 20 provinces and cities came to Wenzhou to make observations, and the impact on them was significant. This was a problem that many people understood clearly at the time." (Wang, 2006)

Yuan Fanglie returned to Hangzhou in 1985, aware of the enormous political risks of the Wenzhou road.

---

[7] See *Wenzhou Daily*, January 15, 1985.

5.4.2. *Systematic summing up of the trial phase (1985–1989)*

In December 1985, Dong Chaocai took over as secretary of the Wenzhou Party Committee. Dong brought with him the intention of correcting the approach of one-sided attention to individual and private economics of the Yuan era, as called for by the Zhejiang Provincial Party Committee. In the first half of his term, he focused on investigation and studying how to develop the SOEs. However, he found upon investigation that for family enterprises in Wenzhou, one yuan input could on average return 10 yuan, whereas for SOEs, 10 yuan input could on average output only one yuan. Despite constantly lending money to SOEs, no sooner had the debts been repaid then back they came asking for more. He thus concluded that state-owned big collective enterprises were big input for low output, with a lot of intermediate consumption and poor economic benefits; whereas the rural private enterprises were low input for big output, with no inter-mediate consumption and good economic returns. The older, larger enterprises in Wenzhou such as the state-owned shipyard had obsolete equipment, heavy debts, were increasingly poorer, and it was difficult for anyone to do a good job as director. It was not a problem of people, but of institutional mechanisms.

At the time he was so perplexed that in April 1986 the State Council Deputy Prime Minister Wan Li came to Wenzhou, affirmed the Wenzhou model and encouraged staying the course. On June 12, Dong received No. 30 of the *Bulletin* of the CCP Central Committee entitled "Main Points of Comrade Bo Yibo's Address to the Central Leadership on Rectifying Party Work in the Countryside", in which Comrade Hu Yaobang spoke on the issue of carrying out China's third major rural strategic alignment (namely, development of the commodity economy, and absorbing the large number of agricultural population moving to industry). Looking at China's actual situation, asked Hu, how was this to be solved in the coming decades? Was it feasible to rely on the state to absorb them? What about a relief approach relying on state expenditures with major loans? Neither seemed feasible. The answer lay in two solutions: first, relying on local funds, i.e., township and village enterprises (TVEs); second, bringing the talent and capital accumulation of individual private operators into full play. Given this, China could develop quickly. On this issue, in

Hu's view, we had to "practice while discussing", and he suggested "first testing in Wenzhou". From this *Bulletin*, the Wenzhou Party Committee learned the following information from the Center: it showed that since the reform and opening up, the path of development of Wenzhou's rural family industries based on individual and private enterprises was considered correct and strategically significant. The central leadership's proposal to test in Wenzhou first was both an affirmation of the development path it had taken, and an indication to continue it.[8] Therefore,

"I [Dong Chaocai] started thinking about adjusting the work, connecting the spirit of the speeches of the central leadership with the actual situation in Wenzhou, and proposed the general idea of further reform and development to be: grasping the 'cow's nose' consisting of the state, collectives and individuals together, and developing individual, private and joint-stock businesses as the economic starting point; firmly relying on peasants, entrepreneurs, and other sectors of small-scale operation and backward production methods liberated from the natural economy to a commodity economy; and promote deepening the reform of the economic structure as a whole, create a mixed development of various forms of ownership, and a new array of urban and rural economic prosperity."[9]

In June 1986, the Zhejiang Provincial Party Committee and Wenzhou Party Committee organized relevant staff to investigate and study in accordance with the spirit of the Center. After more than two months of investigation and study, an initial pilot program was formed. On August 14, the General Office of the Zhejiang Party Committee carried out a task discussion of the program proposed by the Wenzhou Party Committee. In September, the *Report on Establishing Pilot Areas in Wenzhou* was officially submitted to the Central Committee and the State Council. The *Report* identified the key point as "adjusting the ownership structure and bringing the role of market mechanisms into full play". The first topic of the pilot was "freeing the development of the individual and private

---

[8] Dong was not aware of Zhao Ziyang's verbal instructions to Yuan Fanglie to set up a pilot area in Wenzhou.

[9] My interview with Dong Chaocai (oral material).

economy and the shares economy". In October 1986, when Wang Fang, secretary of the Zhejiang Provincial Party Committee, was attending meetings in Beijing, he turned to Deputy Premier Wan Li for instructions on the Wenzhou pilot area. Wan Li held that the program proposed in the *Report on Establishing Pilot Areas in Wenzhou* was feasible, and "should be acted upon boldly". On returning from Beijing, Wang Fang conveyed Wan Li's instructions to the Wenzhou Party Committee. Accordingly, the Party decided to hold a Municipal Party Committee work meeting from November 7–13, 1986, to relay the contents of the Zhejiang Party Committee's *Report on Establishing Pilot Areas in Wenzhou* to the Party and State Council, and to begin preparatory work to plan the pilot project in detail. In September 1987, the State Council officially approved Wenzhou as one of the first 12 rural pilot reforms nationally, and confirmed Wenzhou as a comprehensive pilot reform area focused on TVE institutional building.

After the establishment of the pilot area, breakthrough of existing systems and policies was allowed. This was a driving force for Wenzhou local government reform and innovation and also a talisman against failure. After all, reform is risky. Failure is sometimes unavoidable, but with the "reform pilot area" logo, the risk was greatly reduced. Having set up the pilot reform platform, the focus of the Wenzhou Party Committee's work was placed on policies and regulations to develop individual, private and joint-stock enterprises. In 1987, eight requirements were formulated, three of the most influential of which were the following:

On August 18, 1987, Wenzhou's *Interim Administrative Provisions for Registered Operations* was officially issued. "Registered Operations" referred to a special mode of operation in which some family industry households and merchants who, because they did not qualify as corporations, lacked the conditions to open bank accounts in order to develop sales channels, affiliate with account-holders who were collective or state-owned enterprises, and pursue various business activities in their name. Promulgating and implementing the *Provisions for Registered Operations* meant that private operators in both urban and rural areas who had no legal corporate status gained legal identity and status, thus enabling the outward expansion of production and management activities, buying in goods and raw materials, and selling local merchandise.

On October 2, 1987, implementation of the *Interim Measures for Private Enterprises in Wenzhou* was approved. Wenzhou started drafting this approach as early as the end of 1986. But as the private sector, characterized by employing workers, was a very sensitive political issue, the state paid no regard to laws and regulations for it. Wenzhou had no legislative power, since the private sector policies and regulations relevant to drafting had to be vetted and approved by provincial-level People's Congresses and People's Governments. Upon being drafted, the *Wenzhou Private Interim Measures* was submitted to the provincial government for approval. The enactment of the *Interim Measures* was of concern to relevant domestic agencies. In October 1987, a four-man delegation from the State Council Legislative Affairs Office visited Wenzhou to conduct an investigation. They argued that the basic principles and main features of the *Interim Measures* was in keeping with the Party's policy, and provided a practical basis for legislative work on the country's private sector.

On November 17 and 18, 1987, following the 13th National Party Congress, the State Council held a forum in Beijing on "China's Private Sector Regulations (for comment)" drafted by the State Council Legislative Affairs Office, to which it invited five Wenzhou participants: Song Wenguang, Pan Piliang, Qu Guiren, Zhang Liecheng and Wang Jindong.

Interim Regulations on Certain Issues of Stock Cooperative Enterprises in Rural Areas was promulgated on November 7, 1987. Given the tremendous political pressure of the "socialist affiliation" issue at the time, joint-stock companies in Wenzhou formed from individual family businesses through the families, associates, etc., were called "joint-stock cooperative enterprises". This was because the shareholders were peasants who had recently left the land to engage in commodity production, and were directly engaged in the firm's productive work or management, i.e., they were both shareholders and workers in them; they were unions of capital and labor, thus sharing the features of shareholding and cooperative systems. By creatively blending cooperative and joint-stock systems to form a new form of business organization, and by bearing the socialist-sounding word "cooperative" in particular, it was easy for the higher levels to interpret Wenzhou's stock cooperative enterprises as essentially socialist. For those lower down, enterprise asset management was relatively flexible, and the defect of flying the flag of convenience of a "Registered Operation" — being unable to dispose of assets at will — could be avoided. Besides benefiting enterprises gaining investment through joint stock, breaking through restrictions on private capital, and expanding economies of scale, it was also beneficial to the protection of private property, and has become a form of business organization acceptable to both higher and lower levels.

The drafting and promulgation of these three policies and regulations was a process of local government reform in which Wenzhou, following the spirit of the Center and local realities, through theoretical and institutional innovation, took the initiative to help people circumvent the barriers of the planned economy system and embark on the road of private marketization. In the pilot zone phase, the Wenzhou Party Committee boldly supported civil reform and innovation. As Party Secretary Dong Chaocai said about founding the urban credit cooperatives:

"In late October 1986, Yang Jiaxing of Lucheng district looked me up to tell me about obstruction from his city's branch of the People's Bank of China when setting up its own urban credit cooperative. He said he was himself a manager of a Lucheng street enterprise, the Huannan Power Plant. In 1984, because of a shortage of funds, it had applied to the bank for a loan, but was told that state banks did not lend to street enterprises. All it could do to meet the short-term emergency at the time was borrow from society at high interest rates. This was a big stimulus to Yang to set up a 'private bank' which would directly serve street enterprises and private entrepreneurs. With various planning inputs, he joined three, then five shareholders in raising 318,000 yuan of share capital which was certified by the Commerce and Industry Bureau, and on October 15, 1986 he acquired a 'temporary business license', rented a newly fitted out three-room, three-storey store on New Peace Street, and chose November 1 as the opening day. On October 28, however, the People's Bank issued a 'business prohibited' order, and he became very anxious. I expressed my sympathy on hearing this, and stated that it was a good idea and offered to support him on the spot. I said, 'Wenzhou is setting up a pilot reform zone. The financial system reform in Wenzhou should let you come in.' However, the governor of the

People's Bank remained firmly opposed, saying that he took care of banks. I said, 'I take care of your Party Group secretary.' He had to give in, although the provincial People's Bank did not agree at the time either. I suggested to first test and see. On November 1, 1986, the Wenzhou Lucheng Urban Credit Cooperative opened as scheduled. The Dongfeng Urban Credit Cooperative was opened at the same time. The Lucheng Credit Cooperative was a joint-stock enterprise mainly providing credit to street enterprises and *getihu*; its interest rates floated, it stayed open on holidays, and it was more flexible in its mechanisms than the state banks. It met with a warm public reception on its opening. After two months of operation, it held savings deposits of over 10 million yuan and had issued 9 million yuan of loans, of which 70 percent were to *getihu*, and it had a 100 percent loan recovery rate. Based on these facts, I often communicated with the leadership of the provincial People's Bank, who eventually issued a 'financial business operating permit' to the Lucheng Credit Society in late December 1989. After this breakthrough with the Lucheng and Dongfeng credit unions, other streets in Lucheng became active in launching them and by 1988 there were a total of 18 urban credit cooperatives playing a major role in promoting private enterprise development in the city."[10]

5.4.3. *Political pressures in a phase of hesitation (1989–1992)*

The progress of the spectacular Wenzhou privatization and marketization reforms was not, however, all smooth sailing. Not only did discrimination continue under various pretexts such as the quality of products, but debate over the socialist affiliation of the Wenzhou model never let up during the Wenzhou pilot reforms.

Before and after 1989, when there were differences in the Central Committee over the choice of how to reform, the Wenzhou model (which had been hugely controversial from the start) naturally become a focus of the conflict, especially after the central leaders who had supported the Wenzhou reforms stepped down. The Wenzhou local government was like

---

[10] My interview with Dong Chaocai (oral material).

a tiny boat in the midst of fierce wind and waves, making little headway in the wild storm. From 1989, due to people at the Center continually raising doubts about Wenzhou's line of development, teams were sent three times by the Zhongnanhai to survey the Wenzhou issue.

In April 1989, a CCPCC National Committee member at the Office of the Zhejiang Provincial Petroleum and Chemical Engineering Department memorialized the Second Session of the Seventh CCPCC National Committee, saying that "since Wenzhou opened its pilot zone, the capitalist influence it brought in has been most serious, with higher prices, serious smuggling and tax evasion, speculation, unhealthy practices of corruption and bribery — everything for the sake of money — resulting in a gap among the people between rich and poor". A four-man team was sent by the Research Office of the State Council to survey Wenzhou on August 4. They never came down on Wenzhou's socialist affiliation, but simply recommended to the State Council that the Wenzhou reform work should continue, and that it should gradually improve.

Between October 25 and November 1, 1989, the State Council Research Office sent a second team to investigate the "Wenzhou model" problem. On December 2, the team issued a *Report on Investigation into Wenzhou Issues*, which stated that the Wenzhou model was not capitalist. In terms of the economic and social development situation, Wenzhou had made tremendous achievements in a decade, which were consistent with overall socialist principles and development objectives. In terms of economic structure and mode of operation, Wenzhou had also undergone a great change in a decade. These changes were, in general, consistent with the overall goals of the general reform and opening-up policy and the socialist planned commodity economy. Nor, from a political perspective, had there been any major problems in Wenzhou.

Between July 7–15, 1991, the State Council Research Office sent a third team to investigate issues of the individual and private economy. After serious careful study, the central investigation team ultimately concluded that the Wenzhou model cannot be called capitalist, although there were some negative factors which should not be ignored.

While the Center did not directly repudiate the Wenzhou model, the successive central investigations placed Wenzhou under enormous pressure. After 1989, the Zhejiang Provincial Party Committee, after refusing to draft a report demanding retraction of the Wenzhou pilot zone, put the

Wenzhou pilot program on a back-burner. Party Secretary Dong Chaocai was also removed from Wenzhou in early 1990. The whole town became very jittery. Private owners felt insecure, ceased activities and shut down their businesses in order to protect themselves. Seeing that things were heading in a bad direction, Fangxing Bank boss Fang Peilin immediately cleared his financial business and closed up shop. Yueqing Liu City Low Voltage Electrics was again rectified. Wenzhou's economic growth declined to almost zero (see Figure 5.1).

After 1990, Dong's successor, Liu Xirong (in office from January 1990 to July 1991), followed precedent on the one hand by continuing to support the development of the private economy in Wenzhou, while on the other hand addressed the socially, rather resonant problem of enterprises in Wenzhou producing "fake and shoddy" products, by carrying out a shake-up and strengthening efforts to standardize stock cooperative enterprises. In July 1991, Wenzhou City implemented an integrated social endowment insurance system for the first time. Liu also proposed "waiting for nothing, relying on nothing and wanting for nothing", and announced that for three years the Wenzhou City Party Committee and government would not buy cars or build housing, but would manfully struggle to build an airport. Through carefully fending off all kinds of political pressure and political risks, he managed to restore the Wenzhou economy despite the difficulties.

Kong Xiangyou (in office from July 1991 to December 1992) succeeded Liu as the city's Party Secretary in July 1991, and was charged with correcting biases. Instructed by the provincial party committee, the current Wenzhou Party Committee and government focused its attention, in reform terms, on guiding the transformation of SOEs and collective backbone enterprises into joint-stock firms. In development terms, it focused its attention on market building, such as construction of the Wenzhou Business Mart and standardization of the market order.

5.4.4. *The government transition after establishment of the market economy (1992 onwards)*

Deng Xiaoping went on a "southern tour" on January 18–February 23, 1992. At the 14th National Party Congress, which was held in Beijing from October 12–18, the reform objective of a socialist market economic system was formally set. The Wenzhou model, featuring thorough privatization and marketization, thereupon achieved affirmation from higher and lower levels nationwide, and the magic spell of the "socialist affiliation" issue which had hovered over the city also disappeared. In December 1992, Zhang Youyu took over as the city's Party Secretary. Given the new situation, the new Party Committee and government resolutely stopped guiding individual private enterprises to become joint-stock cooperatives, and in the second half of 1993 proposed a "second venture" strategy, namely to refocus work on the "358 Quality Market Building Project" to upgrade the quality of Wenzhou products, take brand building seriously, and increase Wenzhou's economic competitiveness.

Marked by the 1994 tax reform, China entered a period of further centralization; state-level reform initiatives gradually replaced the autonomous trial and error of local governments and the space for institutional innovation by local governments was greatly compressed. After a soft landing in 1996, Wenzhou economic growth began a period of stable growth. With implementation of the "Develop the West" strategy, many experts and leaders in Beijing called for the West to learn from Wenzhou, whose road of thorough privatization and marketization gained further positive affirmation, setting off another nationwide Wenzhou craze. Following the nationwide all-round opening up, more visitors than ever swarmed to Wenzhou to gain experience and attract investment. Using their previously accumulated capital, Wenzhou enterprises actively invested in and expanded throughout the country. They built markets and took part in SOE restructuring, replicating the Wenzhou model throughout the country. After inspecting Wenzhou in 1998, Wu Jinglian pointed out that in Wenzhou, it was mainly small and medium-sized private enterprises that were competitive: "Wenzhou allows me to conclude that strong vibrant SME groups which formed in some places will soon, if we take measures to support their development and actively guide them, form some large or small 'growth poles'." The demand created by their investment and expansion activities will drive the further expansion of their own production and the economic recovery of other areas, thus stimulating a virtuous cycle of mutual stimulation of supply and demand. This is what we have to strive to achieve.

5.5. Conclusion

After systematically reviewing the history of the reforms in Wenzhou, we find that, given China's unified political structure, Wenzhou's local government had an action choice function almost identical to that of other local governments, but made different reform choices. The differences in these key variables led to the Wenzhou local government's ability to gain the benefit of a higher yield target only by taking the choice of reform action of, unlike other local governments, encouraging the development of individual private enterprises. In China's gradual reform process of "crossing the river by feeling the stones", Wenzhou's bold trial and error reforms based on non-government market-oriented privatization and resulting economic performance showed the central leadership of China a viable path of reform and development in which "the Center takes no money and the people get rich". Setting up the pilot zone not only expanded the Wenzhou local government's space for choice of reform action, it further reduced the friction costs and coefficient of risk of failure of the reforms, thereby encouraging Wenzhou's local government to take bolder reform measures.

In the process of reform and opening up, the people of Wenzhou advanced wave after wave to develop the individual private economy and break the constraints of the old planned economy system, and to promote further reform of local government, precisely because they faced a crisis of life and death and were imbued with a powerful sense of democracy and rebel spirit of boldly striking at the old system.

Given China's politics of grand unification, politicians not only need to immerse themselves at the grassroots level to grasp and gather the actual situation, they also need the vision to drive and master the overall reform situation, and thus greatly reduce local government's costs and risks of reform and so advance it.

The various levels of local government, situated between the populace and the Center, is the core force of reform. Its attitude to reform depends on its ability to grasp the spirit of the central authorities, and its level of understanding of local realities. The value concepts, personal qualities and governing skills of the major local government leaders play important roles in the smooth progress of reform.

References

Dong, Fureng and Renwei Zhao (1986). "Wenzhou Rural Commodity Economy: Investigation of the Road of Modernization in China's Rural Areas", *Economic Research*, No. 6.

Du, Runsheng (2000). "Interpreting the Wenzhou Model", *China Business Times*, July 11.

Fei, Xiaotong (1986). "Wenzhou OK", *Liaowang*, pp. 20–22.

Liu, Alan P.L. (1992). "The Wenzhou Model of Development and China's Modernization", *Asian Survey*, Vol. 32, No. 8, pp. 696–711.

Nolan, Peter and Fureng Dong (1990). *Market Forces in China: Competition and Small Business — The Wenzhou Debate*. London: Zed Books Ltd.

Parris, Kristen (1993). "Local Initiative and National Reform: The Wenzhou Model of Development", *The China Quarterly*, No. 134, June, pp. 242–263.

Shi, Jinchuan and Kangdui Zhu (2002). *Studies on the Wenzhou Model: Retrospect and Prospect.*

Wang, Fang (2006). *Memoirs*. Hangzhou: Zhejiang People's Publishing House.

Zhang, Renshou (1994). "Wenzhou Model: Firms, Markets and the Government Functions of the New Changes", *Zhejiang Journal*, No. 3.

Zhang, Zhiheng (1998). *Annals of Wenzhou City*. Beijing: Zhonghua.

CHAPTER 6

THE PROCESS OF ESTABLISHING AND EXTENDING DIRECT ELECTIONS IN RURAL CHINA

Wang Zhenyao*

6.1. Setting a Stable Direction for Political Reform

Household contracting was implemented in China as a fairly thorough economic institution for how to structurally adjust rural grassroots organizations, define the state's political relationship to the peasantry, and mobilize a transformation of the traditional system of political participation towards the rule of law — these were the major issues facing rural reform in the mid-1980s.

The *Constitution*, promulgated in 1982, provided that the village committee was an autonomous organization, with Directors, Deputy Directors

---

* Wang Zhenyao worked in the Rural Policy Research Office of the CCP Central Committee between 1986 and 1988, where he was responsible for building rural grassroots organizations. In early 1989, he was transferred to be Director of the Grassroots Politics Division of the Rural Division of the Ministry of Civil Affairs. Made Deputy Director of the Division in 1994, he began to direct the comprehensive work of the Division in 1996. In June 1997, he transferred to be Secretary of the Grassroots Political Construction Division. He has long been directly responsible for the administrative direction of rural elections. Currently, he is the Director-General of the Bureau of Social Welfare and Charity of the Ministry of Civil Affairs. This chapter gives an account of some basic processes involved in setting up the village direct election system, the largest in human history. After about two decades of experimentation, grassroots elections have been implemented nationwide and about 900 million farmers currently vote for their village leaders.

and members elected by the residents. The *Law on the Organization of Villagers' Committees (Trial)*, promulgated in 1987, further stipulated that village committees were to be directly elected by the villagers for a term of three years.

The orientation of development toward rural democratization set by the central government was marked by a clear policy choice. Given legal safeguards, rural grassroots democratization could be promoted in stable conditions by an administrative, and in particular, top-down guidance system.

6.2. Choice of the Gradualist Path

While the People's Commune system had provided that production brigade cadres be democratically elected, since the mobilization system relied more on political campaigns, such mobilization-type elections paid attention neither to building specific electoral procedures, nor to strictly defining cadres' terms of office. Once elections were enacted under the rule of law, mobilization-type election would become an inertial obstacle.

In 1986, the NPC Standing Committee began discussing the *Organic Law of Village Committees*. At that time, two highly controversial views were dominant: one was to implement villager autonomy, introducing direct elections in rural areas, and developing rural democracy. Another view opposed this, arguing that it was out of keeping with China's national conditions; the *suzhi* (quality) of the peasants was too low and democracy was impracticable. Eventually, after being discussed in the NPC for more than a year, thanks to strong support from NPC Chairman Peng Zhen, the *Organic Law of Village Committees* was adopted by the NPC Standing Committee, albeit on a "trial basis". Peng Zhen made a famous speech at the 23rd meeting of the 16th National People's Congress on November 23, 1987, arguing that implementing villager autonomy and grassroots direct democracy was a major reform of the country's political system; the implementation of rural democracy was to be encouraged, and the people's representative capacity would be improved through training and practice. This speech set the political tone for direct elections for village committees. Then, in 1988, the Ministry of Civil Affairs officially established the Grassroots Political Construction Division, whose

Director was the then Minister, Mr. Li Xueju. A Rural Department within it was responsible for implementing the *Organic Law of Village Committees*; it was my good fortune to become the first Director of this Department.

The transformation of historical tradition is very difficult. Despite the clear support of Peng Zhen, after the political turmoil in 1989, villager autonomy became a controversial issue. Many people still thought that by changing the village committee into an administrative organization, with village cadres directly appointed by the township government, implementation of government policy would be guaranteed. Some extremists even remarked that "the peasants have no capacity for autonomy: even if they want it we shouldn't give it to them." Faced with this challenge, Peng Zhen remained firmly in support of villager autonomy. He invited leaders of the Ministry of Civil Affairs to go to their own homes and ask about issues of village autonomy. Given this, the Ministry organized a thematic survey of rural grassroots organizations in November 1989. I led a work group to Heilongjiang, where I carried out a field survey of three types of organizations in rural parts of the province. We found that the traditional means of strengthening the building of grassroots organizations in rural areas took the mistaken road of formalization; setting up administrative office-type organizations made relations between grassroots cadres and the masses tenser than ever. However, in areas widely promoting democracy and autonomy, all achieved an excellent situation as regards cadre–mass relations and rural work. Our survey report recommended in this respect that the key to the problem lay in the timely adjustment of political relations between the Party and state with the peasants, and villager autonomy should be developed to promote rural direct elections. Bo Yibo, then Deputy Director of the Central Advisory Committee, gave this investigation report a high appraisal. Overall, the central core leadership adopted an accepting and supportive attitude toward villager autonomy.

How could the central core leadership's political attitude and the law become basic policy in the regions? Actually, in China, due to great regional differences, there are imbalances between the grasp of local realities and the understanding of central government policy. A considerable number of localities actually have a positive attitude toward villagers' direct elections. For example, in 1988 in Liaoning, Shandong, Fujian, and other places, village committee elections were actively organized in a number of counties, which gained some experience, showing that they could be organized in the countryside, with good social effects. By the end of 1989, 14 provinces, autonomous regions and municipalities all around the nation had begun legally electing rural cadres on a trial basis. Also, People's Congress Standing Committees in six provinces (Fujian, Zhejiang, Gansu, Hubei, Guizhou and Hunan) had developed their own approaches to implementing the *Organic Law of Village Committees*. At the local level, Laixi County in Shandong promoted the construction of rural Party branches and organizations with a fundamental policy of democratic elections. The county's Party Committee Secretary, Zhang Chengtang, argued that after the adoption of household contracting in the economy, grassroots administration politically needed to implement "returning rights to the people" and promote democracy. The Ministry of Civil Affairs' Grassroots Political Construction Division argued that the Laixi experience was comprehensive, and could guide the building of rural organizations nationally. It recommended that the Central Policy Research Office, the Central Organization Department, the National Women's Federation and other units hold an on-the-site meeting in Laixi, for Laixi to promote its experience and exchange others from around the country.

In August 1990, relevant central agencies held a national conference on building village-level organizations in Laixi. Song Ping, then a member of the Politburo Standing Committee, attended the meeting and delivered a speech on the question of whether villager autonomy should be carried out. His answer was not to spend time arguing; a law had already been drawn up, so we should conscientiously implement it. During the meeting, regions like Liaoning and Fujian presented their experiences in promoting direct elections of village committees. Central Document No. 19, issued after the conference, pointed out that every county must choose from several to a dozen of village elections for village autonomy demonstration activities, in order to gain experience and establish models. The Laixi meeting can be called a highly significant milestone in the history of direct elections of village committees. It created basically unified thinking among Party and government leading cadres, set the direction for steadily advancing direct village elections, and objectively selected the strategy for the gradual development of grass-roots democracy by guiding the localities to develop village autonomy, and in particular, activities to demonstrate direct village elections.

6.3. Popularizing Direct Elections: The Driving Force of Villager Self-Government Demonstration Activities

After a strategy of gradual development has been set, there is in fact a choice among a variety of scenarios for organizing its implementation. If an approach of allowing arbitrary implementation by the localities is selected without unified national deployment, it may lead to all kinds of differences, so that the elections promote a state of serious imbalance. At that time, the work of the Grassroots Political Construction Division was focused on popularizing the law, because only by letting all the villagers in each locality into the election process could the term of office of village committees be established, so that they would constantly improve their quality by virtue of being elected to three-year terms. Hence, in the early establishment of an electoral system, popularization is very impor-tant: without it, there is no quality to be raised; it is the foundation of raising anything. Especially when promoting rural elections in a country lacking a democratic tradition, established term of office for village cadres is a revolution in itself. Given the importance of the term of office in guiding local village committee elections, the Ministry of Civil Affairs took the approach of firstly popularizing, then raising the quality.

In the strategy of gradual development, how can a direct election system be quickly popularized? On the basis of Central Document No. 19, the Ministry of Civil Affairs issued a nationwide circular, requiring each province, autonomous region and municipality to complete a schedule of villager autonomy demonstration activities before the end of 1990, with provinces focusing on villager autonomy demonstration counties, local-ities focusing on villager autonomy model townships, and counties focusing on villager autonomy model villages. The Ministry of Civil Affairs decided to set Laixi County as the national villager autonomy demonstration county. The Document also made the same request of localities that were not so positive toward direct villager elections, the basic logic being that if you thought that conditions for villager autonomy were not ripe, then could a county generally have one village implementing autonomy? In one locality, could there be one township that explored it? Within the scope of a province, could there be one county carrying out exploration? The difference with this approach compared to the general run of pilot projects was that the Document required pilots to be set up in each province, region and county, so that demonstration activities were actually started across the board. None of the localities could adopt a wait-and-see attitude.

To implement the Document on villager autonomy models, all localities were to report on the model counties, townships and villages they had set up, and formulate plans to achieve results as soon as possible. As a result, in 1991, the localities nominated some 59 village autonomy model counties (some provinces identified as many as four).

What was to be the focus of villager autonomy? In the beginning, it was defined by law as self-management, self-education and self-service, but in practice these were difficult to operate. In order to set up policy norms that would be easier to operate, Li Xueju, Director of the Grassroots Political Construction Division, conducted a survey in Zhangqiu, Shandong, in the spring of 1991. His report pointed out more systematically that achieving villager autonomy in a village could be summarized as follows: formulate a charter for democratic elections, decision-making, and management in accordance with the law — i.e., put in place procedures for villager citizens directly electing village committee cadres to solve the problem of democratic elections; implement a villager representative system to solve the problem of democratic decision-making; and formulate a villager autonomy charter to solve the problem of democratic management. Carrying out villager autonomy in China therefore began with a certain operability, meaning the law had a work system with which to take root. In order to standardize and popularize the policy of building village committees nationwide, the Ministry of Civil Affairs held three national demonstration workshops on villager autonomy in Laixi in the autumn of 1991, to launch the training of Civil Affairs Bureau cadres, especially those in villager autonomy demonstration counties. The Ministry of Civil Affairs in Beijing held a national forum on villager autonomy demonstration work in late 1991. All government leaders from villager autonomy demonstration counties and cities attended this forum and exchanged their various approaches in a great promotion of the national villager autonomy demonstration activities.

In August 1992, the Central Policy Research Office, the Central Organization Department, the Ministry of Justice, and the Ministry of Civil Affairs held a national democratic village management meeting in Shandong. Doje Cering, the Minister of Civil Affairs, pointed out at this meeting that villager autonomy included the rights to vote and to stand for election, decision-making, management and supervision; villager autonomy must be institutionally safeguarded; counties should develop "approaches for direct election of Village Committee cadres" and develop guidance suggestions for villager representative meetings and villager autonomy charters; townships should develop detailed rules to guide the work of the village committees; and villages should set up representative meeting institutions and develop charters of villager autonomy. This meeting was another great impetus towards holding village committee elections.

By this time, holding direct village elections to carry out the *Organic Law of Village Committees* had become a major social activity. By the end of 1992, Standing Committees of the People's Congress of 22 provinces, autonomous regions and municipalities around the country had formulated approaches to implementing this Law, and all the localities had reported completion of a first round of village committee elections to the Ministry of Civil Affairs. In other words, over the five years from 1988 to 1992, although the phenomenon was not yet unified, village committee elections had begun to be unified in form. Even localities that had not formulated regulations for village elections had also organized a local election to give the village basic political legitimacy. Under such circumstances, various localities with inconsistent attitudes to holding direct village elections gradually began to join the ranks of those holding them consistently.

Note that the manifestation of the gradual strategy in the process of popularizing direct village elections was not to force consistency everywhere: neither the pace nor the approach had to be the same. The degree of democracy in the elections differed even more — certain places even retained the traditional electoral method of a show of hands, while localities where progress was faster established competitive electoral systems.

Such a wave propagation approach retained differences, and in fact encouraged local creativity, and conformed well with the style of "gradual promotion, carry one out when the conditions are ripe, carry it out in a group when the conditions are mature, keep up preparations when the conditions are immature too, and carry on working", advocated by Peng Zhen. The Ministry of Civil Affairs did not stay in a *laissez-faire* state as regards local elections, but gave the localities clear policy development orientation through a variety of methods and measures. After five years of effort, direct elections were basically popularized nationwide. It should be said that this was the first stage of developing direct elections in rural China. The focus of this phase was popularizing the tenure system and implanting the three-year term of village committees in rural society. Through this way, the concept of direct elections began to enter political life in rural areas.

6.4. Exploration in Establishing the Direct Election System: Discovery and Promotion of the "Sea Voting" System

The key to democratic elections is building an impartial electoral process. China lacks a tradition of democratic elections or experience of building the electoral process. Success or failure in direct village elections is determined by how a fairly unified national system for a democratic electoral process, which meets with voter approval, can be rapidly set up and improved by drawing lessons from it.

After the countryside had universally completed the first round of direct elections, some localities wanted the second round of elections very quickly carried out. In the first round of the electoral process, some areas had quite a good election experience, while many problems were revealed in other areas. The most salient problem was that direct village elections involved the villagers' interest relations, which had become tortuously complicated in rural society ever since household contracting. Villagers hoped to express their interests by electing the village committee, which meant the latter could not be callously turned into mere formalities, with ballots filled in at random. If the electoral process was not impartial, transparent or sound, more open conflicts would occur, sometimes even escalating into group incidents. Under such circumstances, the effectiveness of constantly promoting the electoral process on a regular basis began to emerge, and all the localities requested the Ministry of Civil Affairs to strengthen its guidance in building the electoral process.

The Grassroots Politics Division took building the electoral process and administrative guidance techniques extremely seriously. We began to set up a project team from 1992 onwards, bringing together concerned experts and scholars to carry out systematic research on village committee elections, villager representative meetings, and building village committees' laws and institutions. Note that the composition of this team was quite unique; it was made up mainly of the staff of administrative agencies. The Rural Division directly organized the research work and all provincial Grassroots Politics Division heads were members of the team, while some concerned scholars took part. It can be said that the team was research-driven by real demands, a search for solutions to problems encountered by administrative agencies in the practice of democracy-building, through academic channels. Rendering it academic was in fact a technological method of handling it. With social phenomena, many problems are dealt with politically. For example, when problems occur in social administration, people usually think of investigating the responsibility of the officials concerned, which is in fact a form of politicization. The politicized approach, however, often fails to enhance all-round construction of administrative systems. This is even more the case with democratic elections: if discussion of the issues is confined to *awareness* of democracy and reduced to whether or not people take it seriously, or even elevated to a debate between reform and conservation, the issue itself can only become more complicated. On the other hand, when the issues are attributed to the building of the electoral process, at the same time discussing specific procedures and techniques, solution of the issues will be simplified, and finding a solution through meticulous academic discussion is made easier.

Technical soundness of the democratic election process requires a great deal of painstaking organizational work. For some years after 1993, the Ministry of Civil Affairs organized a series of important activities that enabled the development of the village committee elections to display a trend of advancing to a higher level every year, forming systematic electoral institutions and procedures. These activities mainly included:

6.4.1. *Comprehensive study of the election throughout the practice and system comparative analysis of the electoral process*

From 1992 to 1993, the villager autonomy research group focused first on the election practice in the various localities. The researchers basically agreed that only democratic systems and methods rooted in Chinese society could have a huge practical impact. Guided by such a philosophy, the national civil affairs system comprehensively collected information on various local electoral systems and methods, and of different incidents occurring in the elections, then later divided the electoral work into the stages of establishing the electoral body, launching the election and voter registration, setting up modes of election, establishing candidates, and casting of ballots with specific comparative analysis, whilst carrying out in-depth exploration of the electoral outcomes, the candidates, the villagers' participation, dismissals and by-elections, illegality and corrective action.

A research report formed from high-level participation in the localities was entitled *Village Committee Election Systems*. In this report, the progress being made in elections around the countryside was listed in some detail, including whether or not relevant regulations had been developed, the format of documents used in the process, the various institutional rules, the formats set for ballots, the mode of voting, the type of campaigning, and so on. Some important conclusions were clearly drawn in the report. It argued, for example, that laws needed to be developed to standardize village committee electoral procedures nationally, to make rules of electoral procedures, ballot formats, and establishment of polling stations more uniform across the country, and to raise the level of organization of the elections. The report also argued that the status of the administrative agencies in guiding elections needed to be highlighted, particularly the guidance of the township level over village elections — township election authorities sent to guide a village must not be considered to hamper its autonomy. Only in this way could equal competition between the candidates in the village be guaranteed. These conclusions set an objective limit to haphazard, unregulated elections, strengthening to an extent the government's responsibility for guiding and standardizing them, and carried a rather strong policy guidance tendency. Going by the electoral practices of other countries, measures to strengthen election administration are necessary for raising electoral justice; without a sound system for the administrative guidance of elections, great confusion will often appear.

The report was made public at a seminar organized by the Grassroots Politics Division of the Ministry of Civil Affairs in the summer of 1993. Those attending were Directors of the provincial Grassroots Politics Divisions, some local grassroots leaders and a handful of experts and scholars. Everyone took part in the discussions, expressing different opinions. Their fairly unified views were eventually included in the study. It should be said that this was a very effective symposium, but also a very effective exchange of experiences in electoral administration work, and was a meeting that combined the two very closely. The results achieved played a decisive role in improving the quality of direct election procedures. The study conducted a systematic summary and analysis of the practical experiences of the localities, and then produced theories that were of great guiding significance in unifying administration of elections in the country. The meeting and the study it published in fact played the role of a training manual, greatly promoting election work in the localities.

6.4.2. The in-depth development of activities demonstrating villager autonomy and establishment of the "sea election" principle

The process of development of direct elections was accompanied by villager autonomy demonstration activities. Prior to 1993, the focus of these demonstration activities started by centering on popularizing village committee elections. Subsequently, the focus shifted to raising the fairness of elections, establishing village committee representatives, and the formulation of laws and institutions related to villager autonomy. In this process, summarizing and promoting the excellent and typical experience of localities in guiding elections was a very important task.

In early 1994, the Ministry of Civil Affairs formally issued the *National Guiding Framework for Demonstrating Villager Autonomy (for Trial Implementation)*. According to the outline, the objectives of villager autonomy demonstration activities were: by 2000, each province, city, county, and township in the land had to establish a villager autonomy demonstration unit which met the standards, and gradually achieve each region (or province) setting up a model villager autonomy county, each county (city) setting up a model villager autonomy township, and each township setting up a model villager autonomy village. Such a time and program for democratic political construction was a first in political institution building.

Meanwhile, the Ministry of Civil Affairs started to review and promote the better typical cases of local electoral guidance work. At this time, three representative models began to be taken seriously. One was Fujian. The *Approaches of Fujian Village Committee Elections* was formulated by the provincial People's Congress Standing Committee in 1990, with a comprehensive amendment in 1993. With the province attaching such importance to electoral work, it was upgraded to the level of special legislation, showing Fujian's higher degree of rural election regulation and also that village elections had made great progress in Fujian. Under the current conditions, the most difficult issue in the elections was how to determine the candidates. In the traditional approach, they were generally determined by the Election Commission. This approach encountered quite a good deal of trouble, however, mainly in that villagers argued that the procedures were opaque and unfair, leaving the election open to manipulation.

On this score, Fujian stipulated that candidates were to be jointly nominated by at least five villagers, and full preparatory consultations (through groups of villagers, the villagers or representatives of the villagers) formed, in accordance with the wishes of the electorate of the official candidates. There was a Fujian traditional characteristic to these requirements, namely "preparatory consultation". However, Fujian further stipulated that the leadership group for village committee elections should brief voters on the candidates, and voters and candidates could brief villager group meetings or villager representative meetings of village committees about the candidates. Such an open briefing facilitated the voters' evaluation of the candidates, and had a competitive nature.

The second local experience was that of Liaoning. This province was the earliest to propagate villagers' experience of direct elections by means of demonstration activities that guided the grassroots to further organize competitive elections. By learning from the experience of Fujian, the more systematically developed *Regulations for Liaoning Village Committee Elections* was passed by the Standing Committee of the Provincial People's Congress in November 1994. Liaoning's *Regulations* were a great step forward from Fujian's, stipulating four ways for the nomination of candidate village committee members: joint nomination by small groups of at least 11 voters; villager self-nomination, seconded by at least 11 voters; nomination by the village Party branch or mass organization; and nomination using the primaries approach to identify a list of candidates. Liaoning also stipulated that after the announcement of the list of nominated candidates, the village Electoral Commission should widely solicit the opinions of voters, and identify formal candidates by means of full preparation and consultation with the villager representative committee on the basis of the opinions of a majority of the villager representatives. The Liaoning provisions effectively abolished "preparatory consultations" in determining candidates, and created a system of voting to choose them. For villager representative committees to determine formal candidates, the views of the majority were required, but how to determine the "majority view"? In practice, only by casting votes. The Liaoning provisions, because they allowed various ways of nominating candidates, whilst also standardizing the procedure for determining official candidates, were of great significance in the history of elections in China.

The third experience was that of "sea elections" in Lishu County in Jilin province. "Sea election" means when village committee members nominate candidates; Party and government leaders at higher levels do not set the tone or draw boxes, but leave the right to nominate candidates completely to the villagers. Each villager constituent writes the names of the candidate village director, deputy director and committee members he or she approves of on a blank nomination paper, and then concentrates on public calling of the names, officially designating the candidates according to the majority principle. This in fact completely merges the nomination and pre-nomination processes, and launches the primaries in the absence of the established candidates. Since candidates are officially decided entirely by those nominated, people in northeast China thought elections like this were like a compass turning at sea, and hence called it a "sea election". About 10 percent of the villages in this county carried out "sea elections" in the village committee election process in early 1992. By early 1995, 336 villages in the county all held "sea elections" and abolished other ways of nominating candidates. The Ministry of Civil Affairs and the Central Party School sent a joint working group to observe elections in this county, and it wrote a special report which was published nationally by the Ministry of Civil Affairs. This report caused a great sensation in the country. Because of disputes that occurred, nominations were a prominent problem affecting many localities. Moreover, the "election" approach created by the Chinese peasants themselves was simple to understand and easy to learn and promote.

The Ministry of Civil Affairs briefed the localities on the respective experiences of Fujian, Liaoning and Lishu County in Jilin, while encouraging everyone to discover their own local experiences and positive creations. In August 1995, the *Guizhou Approaches to Village Committee Elections* was adopted by the Standing Committee of the provincial People's Congress. It stipulated that after publication of the list of village committee nominees, fully prepared by the voters' group, discussion and consultation of the official candidates would be determined by the Village Election Committee in accordance with the majority of voters. This provision also began to standardize procedures for selecting official candidates.

In late 1995, the Ministry of Civil Affairs launched activities recognizing model counties for villager autonomy, officially naming 60 demonstration counties (and cities or districts) for villager autonomy nationally. These advanced units came to Beijing to participate in the national recognition meeting and to exchange experiences. The "sea election" experience of Lishu presented at the meeting had especially great national influence. Thus, a new electoral institution — the "sea election" — quickly started to gain national endorsement. Those people guiding elections began to generally feel that, without a "sea election", elections may not be fair.

The impact of "sea election" on the electoral system can be seen from electoral regulations of some localities. In November 1996, the Standing Committee of the People's Congresses of Hebei and Hunan adopted formal approaches for electing village committees. The Hebei approach stipulated that the pre-selection approach could be used to determine the official candidates according to the number of votes. The Hunan approach further provided that where the number of candidates nominated for the village committee exceeded the formal number of the candidates, the villager representative meeting and villagers' meeting convened by the village election committee would conduct primaries, and officially confirm candidates according to the number of votes they received.

The method of determining official candidates is the core of the electoral system. If the procedures for confirming official candidates are not transparent and public, the election will not seem very fair. After the village committee election system was popularized, because of strong demand and serious organization by the locality concerned, the regulations and institutions for determining pre-selection of formal candidates were rapidly adopted nationally, which had decisive significance for the integrity of the direct election system.

6.5. Development of Key Election Techniques: Establishing and Universalizing Secret Ballots

Is administrative guidance of elections a technique? Is there a key technique at its core? For many people, elections are politics pure and simple, and it is therefore unnecessary to talk about organizational techniques. For instance, should elections set up polling stations as the sole places where ballots can be received and filled out? Should voters queue up to get their ballot, or wait for the electoral staff to come to the voters' seat and issue a ballot? Must ballots be completed independently and other people prevented from watching this process? These problems may seem insignificant to some: they may argue that according to the principles of democracy, whoever wants to do something should do it, whoever wants to organize elections in a particular way should be able to, and someone wanting to fill in a ballot in a particular way can do so. Voters should not be forced to queue up to get their ballot, or asked to enter some secret zone to fill in their ballot. However, the result of organizing rural elections based on this logic would be similar to candidates and their representatives collectively taking their ballots, and publicly supervising voters on how to fill them in. Facts have proven that electoral administration is a very important technique: if appropriate technologies are lacking at key stages, democratic elections could become phony manipulations, and their outcomes would be seen as unfair.

After two electoral terms, the contradictions of technical backwardness in rural electoral work had become ever more noticeable. During this period, the Party and the country's macroeconomic policies affirmed that democratic elections clearly going ahead called for further advances, and that the political environment was very favorable for direct villager election institution building. In October 1994, the CCP Central Committee held a rural work conference on building grassroots organizations, subsequently issuing the *CCP Central Committee Notification on Strengthening the Building of Rural Grassroots Organizations*, which explicitly required adherence to democratic election of village committee members, and for the elections to abide by the law, strengthen respect for the democratic rights of the villagers, and resolutely oppose and correct illegal and irregular activities in elections. Also during this period, the Grassroots Political Construction Division conducted systematic research on the national system of villager representative meetings, and published a special report entitled *The Village Representatives System*. It held a seminar on the topic and further promoted raising the technical standards of administration and management of officials in all localities in charge of rural organization building.

Early in 1994, following many requests, the Ministry of Civil Affairs decided to revise the *Organic Law of Village Committees* and standardize electoral work in all localities. In June 1995, the Ministry of Civil Affairs held a meeting to discuss and agree in principle to the draft *Organic Law of Village Committees (Amendment Bill)*. While revising, we all grasped more clearly that the electoral process is a process of highly procedural and technical work, some operational aspects of which had to be clearly stipulated in the Law.

In 1995, pulling together the amendments to the Law, the Grassroots Politics Division once again specially organized systematic research into laws and institutions for village committees, from basic national laws to local regulations and relevant provisions of cities, counties and townships (in particular, the villager autonomy statutes formulated in the villages), carrying out comprehensive systematic study and once again publishing a special report. The Division later held a seminar to analyze and draw conclusions on the state of implementation of the Law. It can be said that the study report indeed conducted a more systematic inspection of the state of implementation of laws and regulations, from detailed provisions to ways of implementing them. Many of the conclusions of the report unified people's understanding of the rule of law and also promoted the idea of building the electoral process.

From 1995 to the second half of 1996, villages in 24 provinces, autonomous regions and municipalities carried out elections for new terms. Having gone through several rounds, contradictions in rural elections were becoming more evident, and the civil affairs system also had more experience in guiding elections. In order to systematically organize large-scale elections, beginning from the first half of 1995, the Division began specially organizing staff to develop unified technical procedures to standardize elections. After repeated study and design, three important results were produced in the second half of 1995:

The Village Committee Election Workflow Chart. This wall chart told the voters and administrative staff organizing the elections colloquially and graphically that one had to queue up for ballots, then enter a private cubicle to fill out the ballot.

Procedures for Election of Village Committee Members of the PRC. This manual contained 10 chapters, with sections on preparing for elections, voter education and election mobilization, voter registration, candidate selection, formal introduction of and competition between candidates, voting, election of villager representatives and small group heads, invalidity and illegality of elections, dismissals and by-elections, inspection and summary. One by one, the chapters standardized the stages of administration. In the chapter on voting, the paragraph on "voting procedures" alone meticulously provided 18 separate procedures, including: taking up of positions by electoral staff; announcing commencement of the election; explaining the ballots and voting methods; checking sealed ballot boxes; voters queuing up to collect ballots; voters reading the ballots and queuing up to enter voting cubicles; independent filling in of ballots; voters casting their ballots; consolidating the ballot boxes; opening the ballot boxes; sorting the ballots; calling and counting the votes cast; announcing the election results, sealing the cast ballots and filling out election result report forms; making the election results public; and issuing notice of election and work certificates.

In the section on "Setting Up Secret Ballot-Filling Cubicles", the *Procedures* state:

> "In voting places and polling stations, in order to ensure voters fill out ballots undisturbed, we must establish private voting cubicles so that they can independently and freely cast their personal votes. The cubicles should be set up making use of what is available.
>
> Where conditions permit, school classrooms can be used, or the cubicles constructed out of suitable materials. Whatever materials are used, there is a single criterion: enabling individual voters to freely fill in their ballots, with others unable to see what they are doing.
>
> Based on different local experiences, the private cubicles are to be set up scientifically according to local conditions. (1) To avoid voters having to wait too long, the cubicles must be set up in proportion to the population, with one for every 50–100 voters. (2) They must be placed in suitable locations, and should generally be close to the place where ballots are received and close to the ballot boxes, so that when voters have received a ballot, they go in by the entrance; then when their ballot is filled out, they leave by the exit and cast the folded ballot into the ballot box. Voters will queue up, enter in turn, and cast their ballot in an orderly fashion."

Model Cases of Village Committee Electoral Work. This was a brief summary of the experiences of various localities, with strong guidance implications for local electoral officials. The model cases were divided into seven parts, including village committee election regulations; notification of electoral work and implementation programs; electoral preparation; determination of and voting for candidates; dealing with electoral illegalities, dismissals and by-elections; scrutiny of elections, review and archiving; and electoral activities and precedents of villager candidature.

Demand for these three resulting products exceeded supply as soon as they were printed, and were quickly referred to and implemented by the localities. As a result, private voting cubicles became necessary facilities and procedures in the electoral process.

Meanwhile, the popularity of the three resulting products also marked the formation of the operating system *guicheng*, which protected the impartiality of the elections in terms of technical institutions, thus advancing direct elections to a new stage.

Early in 1996, the Ministry of Civil Affairs issued a *Notification Regarding Village Committee Electoral Work*, which required localities — with the provinces as units — to unify their electoral arrangements, length of term, and electoral forms. In August, the Grassroots Politics Division held a national meeting to exchange experiences on village committee elections in Weichang County, Hebei, which fully recognized the importance of building an organizational election process.

In November 1998, the *PRC Organic Law of Village Committees* was formally adopted by the National People's Congress Standing Committee, Article 14 of which provided that for village committee elections, villagers having the right to vote would directly nominate the candidates. Furthermore, at the time of the election, private voting cubicles would be set up. These provisions therefore indicated that "sea votes" and secret ballots were fully integrated into the national laws, and were systematically institutionally protected. Also, the *Organic Law of Village Committees* was no longer a pilot program, thus demonstrating that, from pilot to formal announcement of implementation, a rural democratic election system marked with Chinese characteristics had been systematically established.

6.6. Impact of the Electoral System on China's Political Development

The whole process of launching the rural grassroots direct election system, lasting from the beginning of the formal trial of the *Organic Law of Village Committees* on June 1, 1988, to the formal promulgation by the Standing Committee of the NPC of the new *Organic Law of Village Committees* in November 1998, took 10 years. To take 10 years to establish a direct election system accepted by peasants in the rural areas of China can be considered a successful case of political reform. From 1998 to 2007, direct elections in the countryside have been tested for nearly 10 years. This experience has shown that the grassroots direct election system, with "sea elections" as a basic characteristic, is accepted by the majority of peasants and recognized by Chinese society, whilst also providing an excellent institutional platform for the solution of various social contradictions in the countryside. Speeches about village administration given by many grassroots candidates with economic construction as the main theme, and comparison and competition between different village governance scenarios, have promoted rural democracy and organic integration of economic and social development.

For a long time, whenever the development of democracy was discussed in China, people always argued that the promotion of democratic elections was hampered by the Chinese peasants' lack of culture. The establishment and development of the rural direct election system shows that the political quality of peasants can no longer be said to be low, because the electoral system could be implemented in the rural areas. In fact, grassroots elections have yet to be universalized in the cities. Although some people also argue that family and clan phenomena still survive in rural elections and, indeed, many aspects still need to be improved in rural elections, it would defy understanding if we had no flaws when organizing rural direct elections in a nation that for thousands of years has lacked democratic tradition. Are there not many imperfections even in many of the countries with centuries of history of direct elections? The rural grassroots direct elections are hence acceptable to a majority of the Chinese community.

The successful experience of rural direct election institution building shows that political reform can be successful using a gradual strategy. Such a strategy requires adopting technical solutions to the problems through political institution building. Successful reform lies in not politicizing technical issues; instead, political issues should be made technical, gradually promoting improvement of the political system through constantly improving procedures and techniques under stable conditions. Gradual reform does not mean going with the flow — the organizers need to have certain organizational talents, and be good at breaking down all kinds of complex political issues into technical procedural issues to be solved ever so gently. They also need to be good at learning from local experience, helping it improve and universalize itself. Gradual reform does not mean long-term pilot projects in limited sectors which the majority of the country awaits eagerly, with the result that expectations for the pilot become too high, and pilot experience becomes hard to generalize. The experience of building rural direct election institutions proves that the relationship between universalizing and improving must be properly handled. In building a somewhat radical institution that the country at large is unfamiliar with, strategies of first universalizing, then enhancing — of enhancing while popularizing, then further popularizing and enhancing, in this way widening regional participation and continuously carrying out repeated testing — should be adopted. These strategies can help instill strong adaptability into the institution, and mobilize everyone's enthusiasm. In fact, in the village committee election process, some places experimented with setting up non-electoral offices or administrative zone organizations, appointing rather than electing. The Ministry of Civil Affairs did not order a stop to this, but allowed the experiment. Eventually, after repeated comparisons, some localities began to disband the village offices and administrative zones, initiating the standardized direct election system. In terms of results, gradual reform, if properly organized, will be better paced and more effective than the "violent storm" approach.

In terms of the trend of historical development, there is no doubt that the rural direct election system will lay down an excellent social foundation for China's democratization. Take for example the following story: the daughter of a peasant family which had taken part in direct elections went to the city to work for a university professor who professionally studied democratization. As it happened, the peasant girl began to describe cases of rural direct elections to the professor, of which he knew nothing. Her account of rural elections made a great impact on him. A peasant lacking any culture telling a professor about rural democracy may be a most telling microcosm of the development of democracy in China. Continued development of the successful democratic tutelage of 900 million peasants will unquestionably raise the democratic standard of the country.

CHAPTER 7

THE HISTORICAL OPPORTUNITY OF THE FISCAL REFORM*

Liu Zhongli[†]

In the spring of 1992, a historic speech given by former leader Deng Xiaoping when touring the south awakened people's awareness of a series of issues. The 14th National Congress of the Chinese Communist Party (14th NCCCP) fully implemented the essence of this speech, asserting that the goal of China's economic reform was to build a socialist market economy. Not only did this point out a clear direction for the systematic implementation of fiscal reform, it provided a precious historical opportunity for the reform as well. As one who lived through the reform, recollecting it seems well worth the effort. I have put together here a brief memoir, selecting a few fragments bearing on the design of the reform.

---

* Liu Zhongli, "Caishui gaige de lishi jiyu" [Historical opportunity for fiscal reform], *Zhongguo Gaige Luntan* [China Reform Forum], December 11, 2008.

[†] China's fiscal reforms started in 1994, and was profoundly significant both for establishing a modern administrative system suitable for the socialist market economy, and for regulating the distributive relationship between the finances of central and regional governments. This chapter is written by former Minister of Finance Liu Zhongli, one of the main implementers of China's reforms. It sums up a decade and more of the successful experience of fiscal reform, considering various alternatives to find a system appropriate to China's socialist market economy, and offers guidance for further improving the system, ordering fiscal allocation between governments, optimizing resource allocation, raising living standards, and building a harmonious society.

7.1. An Opportunity Not to be Missed

In the 30 years between the founding of the PRC and the reforms, a highly centralized planned economy was adopted. In administrative terms, the fiscal system was likewise characterized by unified fund collection and allocation. While, given the historical circumstances, this system played a positive role, the vitality of economic growth was dampened by over-centralization and rigid controls. Maximizing economic vitality, therefore, was bound to become the main goal of reform and opening up, and the logical starting point of fiscal reform. These assumptions are confirmed by facts: economic reform has from the outset been led by fiscal reform; there could be no reform without reference to the fiscal dimension.

In the early reform phase, fiscal reform was oriented towards promoting the participation of regional governments and enterprises, and centered around decentralizing fiscal power and relinquishing interests. From 1980 to 1993, the fiscal relationship between the central and regional governments underwent three stages: dividing revenue and expenditure between the central and local governments and allocating financial responsibilities according to the level of government; defining tax categories, verifying revenue and expenditure, and allocating financial responsibilities according to the level of government; and, finally, direct state control over finances. The fiscal relationship between the central government and enterprises changed according to the following stages: expanding corporate autonomy; unregulated tax breaks; and finally, the contracted responsibility system in management, that is, enterprises assuming full fiscal responsibility. Both cases ended up with one party holding *da baogan* (overall fiscal control).

The *da baogan* fiscal system certainly played a certain positive role in promoting the vitality of regions and firms. But the net effect of this kind of control by the Center over the regions was to throttle national fiscal income. Well-off regions would be inclined to under-tax in order to avoid paying additional taxes to the central government. For example, if a 4 percent growth cap were put on the fiscal income of a certain region, the local government would refrain from collecting taxes when that limit was reached, as the additional amount would have to be split with the central government. In another example, the government set the fiscal income of a region in 1988 as a base; any growth in fiscal income would be split 50–50 between the central and local governments. In order to avoid handing money to the central government, fiscal income saw near to no growth during the whole period of that fiscal arrangement. It was the same case with enterprises. In the execution of contracted management, enterprises profited when business was good, but the government was saddled with any losses, leading to a lack of safeguards for national fiscal income (see discussion below).

Such arrangements resulted in tax resources drying up and weak growth of fiscal income. The ratio of fiscal income to total GDP and the ratio of central fiscal income to the national total (collectively known as the "two ratios") was dropping from year to year. The fiscal situation was headed for a crisis, especially at the Center and in the less developed regions. Several measures were suggested to relieve the fiscal crisis. One was to supplement taxes with fees. Central revenue streams, weakened by rate cuts and downward transfers of responsibility, needed to be bolstered. A "Key Construction Fund for Energy and Transportation" was put in place in the 1980s, and a "Budget Regulation Fund" in 1989. Both of these funds were aimed at balancing the budget. Another measure was setting up loans from regional governments to the central budget. In actual fact, this arrangement was the same as asking regional governments to contribute towards central fiscal expenditures. Three such loans were made, but it was clear that they would never be paid back. As for the effect of these measures, even well-off regional governments were unwilling to make generous gratuitous contributions, and the integrity of the central budget was compromised. These measures dealt only with the short-term symptoms rather than the root causes of the fiscal troubles. Furthermore, implementing these measures on a long-term basis would place the central government, regional governments and enterprises in a cut-throat push-and-shove.

Faced with this grim situation the government, starting in 1987, tried repeatedly to drive the reform of the fiscal management system forward. Not only did these efforts hamper promoting reform, they replaced the existing rules with even more unregulated delegation of fiscal power and profit seeking. In the end, speeches made by Deng Xiaoping during his 1992 "southern tour", followed by the resolution of the 14th National

Congress of the Chinese Communist Party (14th NCCCP, 1992) to launch a "socialist market economy", made possible the drive forward with reforms that had been on the agenda of the financial department for years.

7.2. Tax Allocation System as the Core

The 1994 fiscal reform involved many aspects, including the taxation system and the tax allocation system; but the latter was the core. The tax allocation system was one in which the fiscal incomes of central and regional governments were allocated according to certain tax categories, completely making over an older, centralized system whereby the central government negotiated with each regional government separately to establish a tailored fiscal arrangement. The objective of reform was to increase the ratio of fiscal income to GDP, and the ratio of the central fiscal income to the national total. Only in this way could the macro-control capability of the central government be strengthened and the long-term stability of the nation maintained. This is also the same method commonly adopted by market economies. But how to allocate the collection of taxes, however, remained a serious issue to be resolved.

In 1993, when plans for reforming the tax allocation system were being made, China's economy was overheated, the investment of fixed assets was out of control, the financial order was in chaos, and there was hyper-inflation. Given these stringent economic conditions, the challenge was to achieve the goal of increasing the "two ratios" while at the same time improving the macro-environment. Great care was therefore devoted to planning the tax categories: taxes indispensible to safeguarding the national interest and implementing macroeconomic control were marked as central taxes; taxes levied from tertiary industry, agriculture and the benefit economy (such as business tax) were marked as regional taxes in order to promote the development of those industries; and consumer tax was marked as an entirely central tax — by imposing this tax on some consumer products under its control, the state sought to prevent regional governments aiming blindly for higher GDP, prevent regional protectionism, and decrease redundant and unnecessary construction. Most lucrative at the time were sales taxes on the manufacturing industry — for the VAT that was marked as a regional tax prior to reform, a tax-sharing system was adopted, with the central government taking 75 percent and the regional government taking the remaining 25 percent; at the same time, the "state-owned" status of resources implied that the state would retain allocation rights over them. But given that most natural resources were concentrated in the central and western regions and that resource-rich provinces were generally fiscally-challenged, most resource taxes were, with a few exceptions such as offshore petrol resources, marked as regional taxes. The allocation of taxes between the central and regional governments was aimed at allocating 60 percent of tax income to the central government.

Of the 60 percent allocated to the central government, half would be for central government expenditures, while the other half would be distributed to regional governments in the form of transfer payments, mainly to under-developed regions. In the first year after the implementation of tax distribution, the central government collected 57 percent of the national tax income. But one of the principles in designing the tax allocation system was to maintain the vested fiscal income of regional governments as at 1993. Taking 1993 as the base year, the total formed by adding the portion of consumer tax handed to the central government and 75 percent of VAT, minus income allocated to the regional governments by the central government after tax distribution, would equal the amount the central government returned to the regional governments through "tax revenue return"; and this number would increase at a certain rate yearly. In allocating increasing income in future, the central government's tax income would in this way increase year by year, while that of the regional government would decrease. In reality, up to then, the degree of tax centralization of the central government had been less than 60 percent, and the ratio of central government expenditure to total expenditure was about the same as that of before the reform, pointing to the fact that the central government had not used tax money collected from regional governments for its own outgoings, but used part of the money for general transfer payments to under-developed areas, and the remaining amount for earmarked expenditures of regional governments, essentially carrying out centrally-directed regional redistribution.

7.3. Allocation Relationship Between the Government and SOEs as Key

The allocation of tax between the government and state-owned enterprises (SOEs) was another important issue in the 1994 fiscal reform. Prior to reform and opening up, China's economy was dominated by public enterprises, of which SOEs formed the core. Non-SOEs developed gradually after the reform; while their numbers remained small, their market characteristics were prominent. The key to reforming the allocation of taxes between state and enterprise therefore lay in the allocation between government and SOEs.

The reform of China's SOEs started with tax cuts and the gradual increase of fiscal independence. Later, due to the success of the contract system in the rural areas, in which remuneration was linked to output, the concept of "contracting" was introduced in urban reforms. Corporate contract system programs were initially carried out on a pilot basis by some SOEs only; and the system was widely adopted in 1986.

The contract system was not without valid points, but it had many shortcomings as well. Firstly, the contractual packages for individual firms were set in one-on-one negotiations, and as there were numerous human factors and no unified standards, it was impossible to avoid different treatment of different enterprises. Secondly, firms' circumstances varied widely from year to year, and with the government powerless to curb the firms, they could choose not to report profits when the going was good, or to fulfill contracts if they suffered losses. As a result, the government would be unable to collect taxes when enterprises profited, but had to bear the losses when they were in the red. The third and most egregious problem was that due to the coexistence of various entities including private companies and foreign-funded enterprises, all enterprises apart from SOEs were marketized. In allocating taxes between government and firms, it obviously ran contrary to market economy principles — which call for justice, fairness and rule of law — for SOEs to be given differential treatment. This was a controversial issue at the time.

Reforming the allocation of tax between government and SOEs had to start with an objective analysis of the circumstances. Compared with non-SOEs, SOEs paid income taxes as high as 55 percent, and after-tax profits had to be handed to the government. Also, as no social security system had yet been established, SOEs had to shoulder a considerable portion of social responsibility including pension and medical care. If those burdens could not be lifted, they would be unable to compete with other enterprises on a level playing field, and the contract system would be faced with much conflict and inequality.

In order to effectively allocate taxes between the government and SOEs and boost corporate vitality, six measures were adopted in the 1994 fiscal reform. The first was to increase depreciation rates and allow accelerated depreciation. The second was for the government to encourage enterprises to increase investment in R&D and technical innovation; expenses firms incurred in technical development would be counted in expenses according to actual expenditures. The third was that for equipment purchased for technical development purposes, that costing below 50,000 RMB would be counted towards expenses, while that costing above 50,000 RMB would be amortized annually into expenses. The fourth was that interest on fixed asset loans could be counted towards expenses. The fifth was to lower the corporate income tax rate from 55 percent to 33 percent. The sixth was an interim measure stipulating that, in specific circumstances, the bulk of older, fully state-owned SOEs registered before 1993 could be exempted from handing over after-tax profits; at the same time, income tax collected from enterprises making only marginal profits would not be returned.

I was persuaded to accept the last of the above measures by then Vice-Premier Zhu Rongji. At the time, I argued that the investor (the boss) of a corporation should receive due reimbursement. Tax money is public income, and profits are dividends of investors. The reasoning Vice-Premier Zhu gave me was that the SOEs of the day had undertaken quite a lot of responsibility for social services, and as a social security system had yet to be established, leaving the after-tax profits to enterprises could help alleviate their burdens. His reasons were correct, and I accepted his suggestion. In recent years, with the gradual improvement of social security, and the transfer of public social functions such as schools and nurseries for employees to the local government, corporate profits have increased dramatically; the government has started to compile capital budgets formally; and the relationship between investors and managers is becoming more regulated.

With the above measures in place, SOEs could finally enjoy the same market status as other enterprises, which was decisive for establishing a modern corporate system as well.

7.4. Setting Bases for the Two Main Tax Rates

The 1994 tax reform was carried out according to systematic design and the principle of considering the overall situation. The reform's guiding principles were clear: to unify the tax laws, levy taxes fairly, simplify the tax system, divide power reasonably, clarify tax distribution, guarantee fiscal income, and put in place a taxation system fitting the demands of a socialist market economy. Sales tax[1] was the key to the entire tax reform, as it made up a large part of the total fiscal income. After the tax reform, sales tax was comprised of VAT, consumer tax and business tax. In the sales tax reform, the VAT reform was the core. After the reform, a uniform production VAT was applied. The product tax that had been included before the reform was abolished, as it was levied repeatedly in multiple production links. There were two main reasons behind choosing production VAT for this reform: one was to avoid affecting fiscal income, especially that of the Center. To achieve this, it was more feasible to use production VAT, as, while it was less scientific compared to the well-regulated consumption VAT, it was nonetheless a big step forward from the traditional sales tax. The other reason was that around 1993, China's economy was in a situation where investment was out of control and hyper-inflation prevailed; a consumption VAT would have had a certain stimulating effect on investment, out of keeping with the stringent fiscal policy of the time. Recombining the product tax and the pre-reform VAT into a new VAT (which now meant something different) was equitable, rational and able to curb price distortions. But opinions differed on how the rate would be set. The Ministry of Finance suggested fixing the tax rate at 18 percent, giving the following reasons. First, in most European countries where VAT was universally levied, the rate usually ranged from 21 percent to 25 percent; set at 18 percent, China's rate would be

---

[1] Translator's note: literally, "circulation tax" (*liuchuan shui*).

relatively low. Second, the 18 percent rate proposed by the Ministry of Finance was calculated on the principle of not increasing corporate burdens, and was the result of analyzing the tax resources of 38,000 large and medium-sized enterprises with tax payment rates of over 80 percent over the course of three years. The nominal rate of the pre-reform product tax was on average 8 percent, with a real rate of 6 percent, and setting the VAT rate at 18 percent would make the post-reform tax collected about the same as that collected under a 6 percent product tax. But the departments in charge of the enterprises requested that the rate be fixed at 16 percent. Given these conflicting opinions, Vice-Premier Zhu appointed me to head the consultations. My strategy was to simplify the problem, and have both sides make some compromises and settle at 17 percent. This decision was approved by the State Council. I recall the director of Shanghai Finance Bureau, Zhou Youdao, calling to tell me that the municipal leaders had asked them to do some simulated calculations with certain enterprises; the results showed that, compared to the pre-reform tax, corporate burdens would decrease under the 17 percent rate. The municipal government therefore approved of it.

The 1994 corporate income tax reform only included domestic enterprises and left foreign enterprises unaccounted for. There is a reason why the corporate income tax rate was fixed at 33 percent. I recall debriefing Comrade Yao Yilin when he asked me specifically whether this rate could be any lower. Since the income tax rate for foreign enterprises at that time was 30 percent, and a 10 percent increase (3 percentage points) could be imposed on top of that by local governments, lowering the rate any more for domestic enterprises would deviate from the principle of fair taxation, the basic one of the market economy. When I think about it now, the reform we presented last year — merging the laws of corporate and income tax — had a legal basis as regards rates, because we adopted the right rate for corporate income tax at the time.

7.5. Establishing Separate State and Regional Tax Bureaus

Before the fiscal reform in 1994, the tax law constraints had become soft. Each level of government — provincial, municipal and county — was authorized to cut taxes. Aside from systemic factors motivating regional governments to keep money in the hands of the people, the tax levying and administrative system was full of loopholes. At that time, the whole country was one single tax system with localized management. Under this system, some regional government officials could cut taxes as they pleased. The lion's share of the taxes cut was supposed to be handed over to the central government. However, regional governments commonly doled out favors, leaving the central government stuck with the bill. The more tax cuts for enterprises, the less money went into the finance departments, and the national treasury would be the worst off. The fiscal system had now reformed the tax allocation system, but if taxes were not separately levied likewise and a reasonable tax levying mechanism established, there would be no institutional guarantee. No matter how well-allocated the tax, the result would be rendered less than satisfactory due to inefficient execution.

Most developed market economies have separate state and regional tax bureaus. For example, the US has federal, state and even local tax bureaus. In Japan, there are not only central and regional tax bureaus, but a specialized tax police force as well. These countries built their taxation systems on the basis of years of experience, so it can be concluded that establishing separate central and regional government tax agencies has centuries of historical support and meets the demands of the tax allocation system.

To meet the needs of *its* tax allocation system, China established tax bureaus on two levels: state and regional. The state bureau implements vertical leadership, and the regional bureaus implement both vertical and horizontal leadership; of the two, the regional bureaus serve the main function.

There was disagreement at the time. It was argued that the separation would lead to increased staffing. What is the present situation, 13 years later? In 1995 the total number of taxation personnel was 734,000, of whom 439,000 worked for the state tax bureau and 295,000 worked for regional tax bureaus. By the end of 2007, the total number of taxation personnel was 748,000, an increase of 14,000 compared to 1995, of whom 352,000 worked for regional tax bureaus, an increase of 57,000 compared to 1995; while 396,000 worked for the state tax bureau, which is a 43,000 decrease. The increase of 57,000 in the number of personnel in regional tax bureaus is justified. It was decided in 1995 to transfer the agricultural tax from the jurisdiction of financial departments to the regional tax bureaus. With this transfer, some regions moved personnel working on agricultural taxes into the regional taxation system, and other regions hired new personnel.

The separation of tax bureaus was an important measure. Without it, levying billions of taxes every year would be simply out of the question. More office buildings were indeed built due to the separation, but the gains indisputably outweighed the losses. More to the point, it prevented at the institutional level the aberration of using other people's money to do one's own favors, regulated the tax levying order, and cleaned up the operating environment of the market economy.

7.6. Two Major Adjustments

Two major adjustments were made to the allocation of tax powers launched in 1994, firstly, in the growth targets set. The tax base of areas unable to meet their targets had to be decreased. Secondly, in the "two taxes returns", the rate of return was now linked to regional, rather than national, average growth rates as previously.

The reason for the first adjustment was change in revenue growth. In the first month of implementation of the 1994 tax distribution, the tax collected increased by 61 percent over the previous year. But the growth rate for February, March and April decreased month by month. Considering the abnormally rapid increase in the last quarter of 1993 (regional fiscal income in the last four months increased by 60 percent, 90 percent, 110 percent and 150 percent respectively, compared to the same period the year before), this would inevitably lead to slow or even negative growth in the second half of the year. As a result, the central government would not only be unable to obtain income, but might have to reimburse regional governments according to the tax return base. A simple solution to this problem would have been for the evaluation team to verify the tax return base, or reduce it by one-third to restore a balanced budget. But after four months of investigation that began in January, none of the "big evaluation teams" had managed to turn up cases of regional governments inflating their incomes to elevate their tax return bases. We subsequently invited some provincial/local fiscal bureau chiefs to discuss methods to offset the decreasing central revenues. Three proposals were put forward. The first was to link tax growth to the growth of regional GDP, making adjustments according to the 1993 tax base. The second was to take a portion of the tax growth of the previous year and make deductions according to the growth rate of the tax base of different provinces. The third was to accept the tax base reported in 1993, but shift income growth targets down, and solve the problem of potential fiscal deficit with increasing income. Comrade Weng Lihua, then director of the Finance Department of Zhejiang province, proposed at this meeting that we should be united and cooperative when dealing with the problem, and set growth targets for the two taxes province by province; this was approved by all present at the meeting. As for how to set growth targets for the two taxes, there were two opinions: the first was to link growth rates with each province's GDP growth rate; the second was to link them with the growth rates of the two taxes in 1993. We all agreed that the first method would lead to a shrinking GDP as provinces would naturally want their tax growth targets to be lower, causing too many adverse effects. We agreed that the second method was more feasible — provinces with higher growth rates in 1993 should have higher targets, and should shoulder more responsibility for the growth of the national fiscal income and make more contributions.

I put together a report on the meeting for the State Council, and the leadership approved our proposals. Vice-Premier Zhu Rongji gave an inspiring address at the national fiscal conference in August 1994, asking the whole nation to stand united and accomplish reform goals with one heart. He also announced the decision of the State Council on the two major adjustments. After in-depth discussions, the State Council came up with the following three suggestions: (1) Set the growth rate for 1994 for the two taxes at 16 percent, one-third of the growth rate of the two taxes nationwide in 1993, with each province setting its own growth rate target at one-third of its previous year's growth rate. (2) Provinces that failed to achieve their growth target should make up the deficit with regional income, and those failing to reach the previous year's tax base should have the base reduced. (3) Where provinces successfully reached their growth targets, the central government should give out tax base returns based on the ratio of 1:0.3 according to the annual growth rate of the two taxes.

For regions that surpassed their growth goals, the additional income would receive a one-time reward: the tax base return factor would be increased from 1:0.3 to 1:0.6. In retrospect, had we then cut the tax return base of all provinces by 30 billion RMB, we could not possibly have collected more than 100 billion RMB in fiscal income every year, let alone the 100 billion or 200 billion RMB that we achieved in later years, and the whole fiscal system reform would have been completely different.

As regards the problem of linking the tax return rates with regional growth rates, the method implemented in 1994 was to set the tax return rate by the same coefficient for all provinces (or regions), based on the national growth rate of the two taxes. The rationale behind this method was that by using the same coefficient, the reimbursement to richer provinces would be relatively lower, while that to poorer provinces would be higher, resulting in a balancing effect. Later, officials from regional governments proposed a province-by-province linkage of tax return coefficients to growth rates. The reasons given were as follows: first, linking the return rate to the province's tax growth rate would embody the principle of efficiency, as provinces with higher growth would receive more, and those with lower growth less reimbursement, eliminating any unfair advantages. Second, this method would encourage local governments to dedicate themselves to the region's production and circulation, not to mention collection of VAT. Third, the central government's fiscal income would increase when more reimbursement was given. It could then give the extra income to slow-developing areas through transfer payments, which would again act to balance income disparities. We thought that this proposal was valuable and made adjustments accordingly. This was the second major adjustment in the execution of the reform, and its significance cannot be underestimated.

Under the guidance of the Communist Party and the State Council, and with the support and cooperation of all provinces, the fiscal reform was initiated on January 1, 1994. The many minor adjustments in its execution aside, on the whole the reform was positive and well-grounded, and its anticipated goals were accomplished. Centered on the tax allocation system, the fiscal reform brought an initial order to the relations between government, enterprises and individuals, and promoted the enthusiasm of all parties. Fiscal income increased significantly, and a mechanism for stable fiscal income growth was set in place. National fiscal income would pass the 1 trillion RMB mark in 1999, 2 trillion RMB in 2003 and 3 trillion RMB in 2005. In 2007, national fiscal income stood at 5.13 trillion RMB, and its proportion in national GDP grew from 12.3 percent in 1993 to 20.6 percent. The tax allocation system also reversed the declining trend of the ratio of central to national fiscal income. This ratio would grow from 22 percent to 54.1 percent between 1993 and 2007. With growth in the central fiscal income, the government's transfer payment capability, especially to the central and western regions, would grow substantially. Currently, transfer payments from the central budget to the central and western regions make up one-third to half of the fiscal expenditure of these regions. The reform experience of over ten years has proved that the decisions made by the CCP and the State Council were correct.

Of course, there are still problems in the fiscal system for a variety of reasons. For instance, regional tax income systems have yet to be established; resource taxes are in need of further reform; and the fiscal income of some regions is still strained. All these problems await solution in future reforms. China is a country with unusually wide discrepancies between regions, and conflicts between the unification of policies and the differences in regional conditions are unavoidable.

Improving living standards and establishing a harmonious society, improving the current fiscal system, ordering the fiscal distribution relationship between governments, and optimizing resource allocation by taking into consideration the special circumstances of our country and summarizing the experiences of over ten years of fiscal reform still remain serious challenges.

CHAPTER 8

FISCAL REFORM: THE ZHEJIANG EXPERIENCE

Weng Lihua*

8.1. Growing the Pie: Local Innovations in Improving Incentives

After the 1994 tax allocation system reform, the Center's capacity for financial transfer payments capability was enhanced. In 1993, the Center's self-sufficiency stood at only about 73 percent; by 2006 this had increased to 205 percent, which was a 132 percent net increase within 13 years, with an average annual increase of 10 percent.

Just as there are two sides to every coin, the tax allocation system reform brought with it a set of problems as well, including imbalances in fiscal power and jurisdiction at all levels of government. In other words, the central government collected a portion of its fiscal income from each province; the provinces did likewise, asking regional and city governments to turn in tax money; they in turn collected money from counties and villages under their jurisdiction. This self-similarity resulted

---

* While the previous chapter reviews the process of fiscal reform from the central government's point of view, this chapter authored by Weng Lihua offers complementary perspectives from the viewpoint of local governments. Weng Lihua was the director of Bureau of Finance in Zhejiang province from 1993 to 2003. He played a key role in implementing direct management of county fiscal affairs by the province and abolishing rural taxations in Zhejiang province. The chapter documents the differences between the central and local governments in the implementation of fiscal reform and stresses the importance of local specific implementation and county autonomy. It also highlights several local innovations in the fiscal reform process that transcend conventions and improve incentives.

in substantial weakening of the fiscal situations of base-level governments, who were increasingly feeling the pinch. The financial
self-sufficiency of some regional governments fell from 102 percent in
1993 to 61 percent in 2006, an average annual decrease of 3.2 percent. In
2005 there were 556 counties and cities with fiscal deficits, which meant
that 27.5 percent of all regional governments were in the red, with a total
deficit of 12.74 billion RMB. According to statistics provided in a report
entitled *Rural Reform and Rural Reconstruction*,[1] the net debt in the fiscal
balance sheet of all villages nationwide in 2002 amounted to 177 billion
RMB, with the average debt held by each village standing at 4 million
RMB. 65 percent of all villages in the country were burdened by debt;
88.2 percent of Hunan province's 2,000 villages were debt-ridden, and the
number in Hubei province was over 95 percent.

For more than two millennia — from the establishment of the system
of controlling counties from the Center in China's Spring and Autumn and
Warring States periods,[2] and after the further consolidation of the county's
dominance through the establishment of the system of prefectures and
counties carried out by Qin Shihuang[3] — the administrative system and
names of counties have remained unchanged. County leaders were, until
the Qing dynasty (1644–1911), always personally appointed by the
emperor. Counties have, up to the present day, dominated China's vast
countryside. The quality of rural construction depends heavily on their
administrative capacity and fiscal strength. The county government
is therefore an extremely important nexus in the system of national
governance.

Thus, after the reform of the tax allocation system, in order to protect
the fiscal stability of base-level governments, Zhejiang's Finance Bureau
decided to take actual circumstances into consideration and establish a
more "flattened" administrative hierarchy, in which counties would be
under the direct jurisdiction of the province instead of city governments.

---

[1] Published jointly by the General Office of State Council Rural Tax Reform Work Team
and the research team for the "Policy Trend of Deepening the Rural Tax Reform" project,
Rural Economy Research Department, State Council Development Research Center.
[2] (770 BC–221 BC).
[3] The First Emperor of Qin (259 BC–210 BC) and unifier of what was to become China.

In this way, procedures would be simplified and the possibility of improper appropriation of tax money avoided. In addition, as Zhejiang's Minister of Finance and a former county and city magistrate, I knew all too well that at the county level, industry structure often centered around a single sector and enterprises were fairly unstable. If the province imposed a tax allocation policy on counties, it would inevitably cause huge turbulence and destabilize industrial revenues. There exist certain differences between Chinese traditional culture and that of the West. In the latter, everything is in black and white — what's yours is yours and what's mine is mine, like drawing a line through the center of a circle dividing it into two separate parts, one side black and the other side white, providing a clear boundary. But in Chinese culture, there are a lot of grey areas — there are two sides to everything and nothing is "completely" right or wrong, just like drawing an "s" curve in a circle (forming a Tai Chi symbol), with some black on the white side and some white on the black side, signifying that there is right within wrong and wrong within right, i.e., nothing is definite. Hence, were provinces to apply traditional Chinese cultural principles to designing the fiscal system and implement a policy to share excess revenue, it would not only help stabilize the counties' revenues, but would be accepted easily as well. The Provincial Finance Bureau evaluated counties according to their geographical position, economic foundation and development potential, categorizing them into the following groups: state-level "poverty" counties, provincial-level "poverty" counties, "island" counties, "peninsula" counties, and average counties. It also set the following ratios for turning in excess income, using fiscal revenues of 1993 as a base number: 20 percent, 15 percent, 10 percent, 5 percent, and 0 percent, respectively.

Zhejiang had experienced financial difficulties back in the 1990s. In 1993, not only did 47 counties report fiscal deficits, but even Hangzhou, the provincial capital, had had to take out loans in order to pay government staff their salaries. During the most difficult time, even provincial government organizations had to scrape up funds to pay their staff. With the implementation of the tax allocation policy during the 1994 fiscal reform, the fiscal situation was made even worse: revenues declined while government duties remained unchanged, miring Zhejiang province's fiscal situation in gloomy prospects. The situation was especially dire in poverty-stricken counties, and it became common for salaries to be unpaid.

In 1994, the Provincial Department of Finance increased subsidies to the 17 "poverty" counties by 55 million RMB on top of the subsidy within the original fiscal system. A total deficit of 122.2 million RMB was nonetheless reported. At the time, given the lack of incentive policies or institutional checks, it was unclear how the Provincial Finance Bureau would go about exploiting each county's potential expenditure cutbacks and increased income.

In order to find a solution to the fiscal deficit problem, as Minister of Finance in Zhejiang, I proposed the financial management concept of "Focusing on people, working smarter, and remaking the financial management mechanism", and led a team of officials from the budget office on visits to more than 20 counties to conduct investigations and solicit suggestions, especially to listen to the frank opinions of county leaders. Through candid dialogues, the provincial government gained a clear understanding of people's rational drive to maximize their own interests, while bringing everyone to the same level in the knowledge of how to improve the fiscal situation. On the surface, the fiscal problem seemed an economic issue, but it is in fact a question of ideas about financial management, in which the most important point is finding how to motivate people through their rightful interests.

In the past, when financial departments provided assistance to poverty-stricken counties, the standard practice was to subsidize them at a set level for a few years, or to set the amount of initial subsidy at the beginning of the year and hand out additional subsidies at the end of the year according to the fiscal situations of each county. This resulted in more funds going to the "child who cries louder" — the more difficult the county's finances, the more subsidies it received, and the further in the red it went, the more it got. This helped propagate the practice of "waiting, relying and demanding", weakening any incentive to make the "pie" bigger. Any county that did so would see its "poverty" status removed, and hence a reduction of the subsidies it received — for which its Party Secretary and Mayor would inevitably be held accountable. When it came to balancing revenue and expenditure, county officials would be even less inclined to make efforts to eliminate imbalances, as doing so would inevitably require cutting back on expenditure on political merit projects, equivalent to "dropping a rock on their own toes" and damaging their career prospects. Even if the Party Secretary and Mayor decided to implement practical measures to balance revenue and outgoings, it would be impractical to assume that other officials such as Executive Committee members or the Deputy Mayor would be on board with the plan. They would be more inclined to approve political merit projects helpful to advancing their own political careers. At the end of the day, leaders are not gods; they are also human beings who have ambitions for either power or fortune. The real problem, therefore, was that the Provincial Finance Bureau was unable to offer any incentives for counties to balance their finances and make the "pie" bigger.

Power and fortune are the two eternal pursuits of human societies. Power can be used as an incentive to encourage human resources departments to achieve better management in exchange for career advancements; but the only feasible incentive for financial departments to manage money more efficiently is money itself. The effort to improve fiscal performance and balance the finances could work only by designing a humanized policy based on "feeding the industrious child more", that showed that both the county and its individual officials would benefit from growing the fiscal pie. The Zhejiang Finance Bureau chose Jinning, an impoverished county, as a sample site and carried out investigations, budget estimations and negotiations. As well as being a small mountainous county, Jinning was also the only county occupied by ethnic minorities in the mid-east region. Above all, the director of its Finance Bureau and other leaders were intelligent and critically-minded people, and hence amenable to rational persuasion.

After a lengthy negotiation process, a policy incorporating incentives and restrictions emerged that was accepted by the impoverished counties. It featured "Two Guarantees and Two Reimbursements".

The "Two Guarantees"[4] were:

(1) a guarantee to balance financial revenue and expenditure;
(2) a guarantee to liquidate deficits run up in the previous year.

---

[4] Under the central government's previous reimbursement policy, there had also been "Two Guarantees", namely guarantees to pay the "Two Taxes".

The "Two Reimbursements" were incentive measures:

(1) increasing institutional subsidies at a ratio of 2:1 relative to the region's revenue growth;
(2) offering personal financial rewards amounting to 5 percent of the region's revenue growth.

The policy was first implemented in the 17 "poverty" counties across the province, with Lishui as the key region. Lishui's regional financial department received reimbursements according to the performance of its nine counties. Under the premise that all nine realized the two guarantees, Zhejiang would hand out 14 percent of the total regional fiscal income as financial funding, and give additional reimbursements equal to 5 percent of the total reimbursement received by the nine counties under its jurisdiction.

The 1995 results saw the policy yielding substantial results. The total fiscal income of the 17 counties grew 34 percent on the year before. Not only did every county achieve balance of revenue and expenditure, there was even some surplus. The results were especially impressive in Wencheng County, a state-level "poverty" county, which used to have an annual fiscal income between 7 million and 8 million RMB. Its fiscal income now grew by 125 percent in 1995, not only clearing the previous year's deficits, but allowing the county to invest 3 million RMB to develop its own assets. Thanks to the county leaders' efforts to manage water and electricity resources, and to convince overseas Chinese from Wenzhou who owned restaurants in Europe to invest in Wencheng, Wencheng's 1996 revenues achieved another 75 percent increase on the year before, realizing a miracle. The Party and government leaders who used to put pressure on the Bureau of Finance, and who aided and abetted counties in reporting financial hardship in order to obtain more government subsidies for their own benefit, also made impressive turnarounds. They did all they could to help the counties achieve the Two Guarantees, and worked side by side with the Bureaus of Finance at provincial and county level. An example of this was in 1994 when Songyang County was 2 million RMB short of balancing the financial revenue and expenditure; the regional Finance Bureau put up the money to help the county achieve balance in order to achieve collective benefits and realize a win-win situation.

With few corporations, the provincial Finance Bureau's fiscal sources were extremely limited. To provide for reimbursements and subsidies, some funding came from the revenues of "poverty" counties, but considerably more came from extra taxes collected from the well-off ones, raising the question of how to encourage the latter to increase revenues and thus support the Finance Bureau. To achieve this, we could no longer use the reimbursement system described above; so we could only use rewards given to the leaders of the well-off counties. This forced us to adopt the measure of "working smarter" and use rewards as bait to encourage county leaders to promote fiscal income growth and hand over more tax money willingly.

Guided by the principle of "Focusing on people, working smarter, and remaking the financial management mechanism", my Bureau started various incentive schemes for leaders of well-functioning counties. In 1994, the provincial government started to reward 300,000 RMB to the financial and tax departments and government leaders of counties with over 100 million RMB in fiscal income, and the incentive was increased by 200,000 RMB for every additional 30 million RMB increase. On the basis of the 1994 reward system, a "Two Guarantees and Two Rewards" scheme was put in place in developed counties in 1997. It featured the same "Two Guarantees" as in the fiscal policy in poverty counties, while the "Two Rewards" comprised incentive schemes: (1) rewarding counties with development funds equal to 4–4.5 percent of additional fiscal income gained, and (2) rewarding individuals with an amount equal to 0.5–1 percent of additional fiscal income gained (renamed "Two Guarantees and One Reimbursement" in 2003).

It is human nature to seek to optimize one's own interests, which was why the fiscal reimbursement policy described above could "work smarter". In addition, as individual incentives linked to fiscal income growth for high-level county government officials had a multiplier of 3.0, which was by far higher than the average 1.0 for financial department officials, it spurred their commitment to improve revenues and gave them the incentive to refrain from corruption.

Apart from restrictions and incentive measures, infusing county government officials with modern concepts of financial management was another main policy. It was an innovation when the Finance Bureau arranged for county officials to take the stage in fiscal forums. From 1994, the province held two fiscal forums for county officials every six months, one for "poverty" counties and the other for developed counties. In these forums, discussions on ways to achieve fiscal goals were carried out from different starting points. According to administrative relations, the Finance Bureau had no authority to hold forums for county government officials and Party leaders. Having formerly been a Deputy Secretary-General for the provincial government, I therefore asked one county to act as host for the first year and to invite officials from other counties to attend. The right to host the second forum was decided by an Olympic-style auction mode, with the winning bid entitled to be host-county for the next forum. The topic of each forum was determined six months in advance to allow time for drafting speeches and other material, all of which had to be vetted and approved by the Financial Research Center before they could be used in the forum. County officials were not allowed to read from a script at the forum, but had to speak off the cuff. All official speeches having been made, I, as director of the Provincial Finance Bureau (and Regional Tax Bureau director as well), would be invited to speak to give guidance for improving the fiscal situation. After further revision, the speeches were submitted to the Financial Research Center and compiled for publication, and all authors would be given royalties according to regulations.

With different topics discussed at each year's forum, the county officials were forced to work hard to brief themselves for their speeches, thus substantially advancing their financial management concepts and enhancing their ability to lead. At the end of each forum, a handover ceremony would be held in which attendants would exchange gifts, much like the flag-passing ceremony at the Olympic Games. The public found this very interesting, and many county officials considered hosting the forums during their tenure a great honor.

During the fall of 1998, Liu Zhongli, then director of the Economic Restructuring Office of the State Council and a former financial minister, led a team of department and bureau officials to the poverty-stricken region of Lishui in Zhejiang to hold a fiscal meeting with the county government officials. During the meeting, Liu highly praised the officials' speeches at the forums, stating that Zhejiang was a rare example in the country for having county officials who were so adept at financial management. Just as in Chinese acupuncture therapy, where only by inserting the needle in the right place can treatment be effective, Zhejiang achieved such great results by focusing on the key area of motivating its officials to improve their financial management.

Zhejiang achieved impressive results by adopting the financial management concept of "Focusing on people, working smarter and remaking the financial management mechanism", implementing the work mode of "focus on both 'poverty' and developed counties, reimburse regional governments for increasing their revenues, and use power and money to motivate", and establishing a fiscal system that incorporated both restrictive and incentive measures. The results achieved were substantial. Firstly, there were no deficits in Zhejiang's financial balance after 1995. Secondly, no instances of late or defaulted salary payments occurred throughout the province. Thirdly, growth in the economic development and fiscal income of poverty counties was promoted. In 1994, the total fiscal income of the 17 poverty counties in Zhejiang was 674.59 million RMB, growing to 849.81 million RMB by 1995. Provincial subsidies to these counties grew from 202.78 million to 263.90 million RMB. Not only did regional government funds increase substantially, but the long-term deficit was finally eliminated. In addition, the province's direct management of counties promoted their economic development and increased fiscal income, promoting Zhejiang in the national ranking of fiscal income from eighth in 1994 to fourth in 2001, and making it a classic case of a geographically small, yet economically strong province.

8.2. Reform Means Transcending Conventions

Reform means transcending conventions — following old rules all the time can never lead to a breakthrough. It was by breaking with convention that Zhejiang had achieved results. Firstly, no formal document was issued in advance of the implementation of the "Two Guarantees and Two Reimbursements" policy. When, as director of the Zhejiang Finance

Bureau, I informed Executive Deputy Governor Chai Songyue of the decision to implement such a measure, he said: "If the trial fails, you can say that you had no knowledge of our plan and it was all my doing; and if we succeed, it wouldn't be too late to write up reports." After one year of the implementation of the policy, great changes were brought about to the poverty counties of the province, making Zhejiang the only province in the entire country to achieve balance of financial revenue and expenditure in all its counties — an impressive achievement at a time when 40 percent of counties in the country were unable to make salary payments on time. At that time, even prosperous provinces such as Guangdong and Jiangsu had many counties that were troubled by fiscal deficits. When a *Xinhua News Agency* reporter got wind of the achievements of Zhejiang, he compiled an internal report for the central government. After reading it, central government officials asked the Central Policy Research Center to find out about the Zhejiang experience. The Zhejiang Finance Bureau filed an initial report with the provincial government, and afterwards the "Two Guarantees and Two Reimbursements" policy made its way into the documents and decisions of Zhejiang's Party committee, the government and the provincial NPC, becoming a jargon term. After a special report on this policy was issued by the Fiscal and Economic Committee of the NPC the following year, it became a substitute for fiscal poverty relief.[5]

Zhejiang's efforts in implementing the direct management of county fiscal affairs by the province and establishing the collaboration between financial departments and regional tax bureaus weathered many obstacles before achieving results. At the beginning of the implementation of direct management of county fiscal affairs by the province, leaders in the State Council did not have any knowledge of the policy. It was not until 1995 when Vice-Premier Zhu Rongji went to Qiandaohu Lake (the New Anjiang Reservoir) to handle the problem of people who had migrated there back in the 1950s that the central government learnt of the policy. At the time, a highway around the lake was under construction to improve production conditions and the migrants' quality of life. The Vice-Premier

---

[5] The "Two Guarantees and Two Rewards" policy implemented in 1997 in developed counties was signed and approved by Chai Songyue as Acting Deputy Governor only, and no formal documents were filed.

proposed that the central government, Zhejiang province and the city of Hangzhou collectively fund the construction project, which would cost a total of 60 million RMB. It was when Hangzhou City government officials reported that Hangzhou could not contribute to the fund since Zhejiang province implemented the direct management of county fiscal affairs that the Vice-Premier learnt of the fact that Zhejiang did not follow state-issued policies that stipulated that counties should fall under the jurisdiction of the city government. Vice-Premier Zhu Rongji then asked Zhejiang's Provincial Party Secretary Li Zemin to immediately make changes to the financial management system to comply with state regulations.

In order to keep the policy going, with the support of provincial Deputy Party Secretary and Deputy Mayor Chai Songyue, I lobbied some senior leaders to convince Party Secretary Li Zemin to continue with it. We sought to persuade him that given a few more years, the results would confirm our fiscal system's rationality. After a year of backing and filling, by which time the whole nation had suffered from fiscal income deficits to the point that even northern Jiangsu and northwestern Guangdong were unable to guarantee making regular salary payments to their government staff, Vice-Premier Zhu Rongji finally stopped pressuring Li Zemin to maintain the policy of the city controlling the county. But what really made Party Secretary Li Zemin relax was an investigation report made by Liu Zhongli when he took up positions as Minister of the State System Reform Office and head of the Special Issues Office. The report positively appraised the results achieved by Zhejiang's Finance Bureau in its decision to manage county fiscal affairs directly, and it proposed that similar policies be implemented throughout the country. Many central government officials, including the State Council Premier Zhu Rongji and Politburo Standing Committee member Hu Jintao, wrote suggestions on the report. When I received a copy of the report from Director Liu Zhongli for examination by the Party Secretary Li Zemin, I let out a sigh of relief.

As discussed in the previous chapter, the State Council passed legislation to establish separate state tax bureaus and regional tax bureaus in place of provincial-level and regional-level tax bureaus, and set the deadline at August 15, 1994 for implementation. The Zhejiang government took into consideration the fact that the establishment of two separate tax bureaus would inevitably increase the number of staff and increase the cost of tax collection, and so decided to set up two separate entities without actually separating the workload in order to avoid excessive inter-bureau coordination and cut costs. Hence, the state and regional tax bureaus in Zhejiang worked in collaboration up until August 1997. Following a scandal over forged value-added tax receipts in the city of Jinhua in Zhejiang, the provincial government came under pressure from the National Tax Bureau to take action, and in June 1997 the provincial Party Committee and the provincial government asked the provincial Party Committee Deputy Secretary and Deputy Prefect to call me to supervise the separation of the tax bureaus. I was, at the time, studying at the Central Party School in Beijing. By mid-July, having finished my studies, I went directly to Changchun to attend the National Fiscal Conference. On returning to Hangzhou as Director of the Zhejiang Finance Bureau, Party Group Secretary and Director of the Zhejiang Tax Bureau, I started to work on separating the tax bureaus. I appointed Qian Baorong (at that time the Deputy Director of the Finance Bureau, a Bureau Party Group member, and Director of the Zhejiang State Tax Bureau) to head the state tax bureau, and appointed Huang Xuming (then a Zhejiang Finance Bureau Party Group member and Deputy Director of the Zhejiang Regional Tax Bureau) to head the regional tax bureau, and the two parties discussed the separation plan through friendly negotiation. In August 1997 the separation of the state tax bureau was complete, and by September all regional tax bureaus were separated. I took into consideration the fact that after the separation of the tax bureaus, the regional bureaus still worked with the Finance Bureau. Special preferential treatment should therefore be given to the newly established state tax bureau. Thus, in the separation plan, it was stipulated that 60 percent of the previous Zhejiang Tax Bureau staff and 70 percent of the total operation fund be allocated to the state tax bureau, and 40 percent of the staff and 30 percent of the operation fund be allocated to the regional tax bureau. In the three years in which the state and regional tax bureaus worked together *de facto*, all tax collection costs were paid out of provincial funds; the fact that the province did not ask for part of the 300 million RMB which the state tax bureau was allocated showed that all parties were willing to work together in a mutually supportive way.

After the separation of the Zhejiang tax bureaus, the regional tax bureaus at the county-level still worked in collaboration with the financial departments, and no *de facto* separation was established. Regional tax bureau leaders implemented a management system incorporating overall management and regional management which was characterized by a streamlined workforce, low costs, easy coordination and high efficiency. It also brought ample opportunities for officials to move from one post to another, avoiding the situation of officials being stuck in one institution. Similarly, the provincial-level financial department and the provincial regional tax bureau also adopted the practice of one leadership in two institutions, with the same team of leaders in charge of both institutions, and implemented unified allocation of personnel.

From 1994, Zhejiang carried out a policy of collaboration between the state and regional tax bureaus, with one team of leaders supervising the operations of both bureaus. By September 1997 the provincial government realized that, while continuing the policy might be advantageous for the overall financial situation, it would also hinder the political advancement of some. Ever since August 1994, the central government and the State Council had heard constant complaints about policies implemented by Chai Songyue and myself in Zhejiang, and we were also criticized by name by a State Council official during the Beidaihe Meeting. The situation reached the point where Chai Songyue told me: "Beijing called to warn me that we would gain nothing by continuing with this policy, and that if we continue to defend it we must be prepared to be dismissed from our positions!"

Time brings everything into perspective. Xiang Huaicheng made the following comments on Zhejiang's special policy at the China Museum of Finance and Taxation on June 19, 2008:

"After implementing the new industrial and commercial taxation system, the tax allocation policy was put forward. According to state regulations, the old tax system was now separated into two systems: a state tax bureau system under direct central government jurisdiction, and a regional tax bureau system managed by regional governments. It can be said that this attempt to implement the tax allocation policy was the first in China's history. In retrospect, the central and regional governments adopted a very prudent attitude to the separation of taxation responsibilities, and departments within the taxation system collaborated very well.

The separation of the tax system could easily have led to conflict, as it is common for a division of duties to cause arguments. But this attempt to separate the tax system went extremely smoothly, and only a few minor conflicts arose. Inevitably there were some problems after the separation of the tax system, but there is ample evidence that the separation led to more efficient tax collection and management. This is especially true for some minor categories of tax, which were neglected when the tax bureaus were preoccupied with the collection of a few main taxes. But after the establishment of regional tax bureaus, more attention was turned to collecting the minor taxes. The results were quite impressive.

The deadline for the separation of tax bureaus was set at August 15, 1994. The regional governments in fact had some doubts about separating the tax bureaus, with Shanghai, Zhejiang and Hainan expressing the most concern. Although tax policies should be unified across the country, in a country as huge as China, it shouldn't be considered a bad thing for a few provinces to stick to some policies of their own that they consider effective. This is an example of taking actual circumstances into consideration, being flexible in our reasoning, and drawing experience from practice. Later on, all provinces except Shanghai and Zhejiang followed the state-issued directive to establish separate tax bureaus. In historical terms, it was because of the different policies carried out in these two jurisdictions, and the efforts made by their respective leaders, that their tax collection and management remained efficient (a result affirmed by the tax income growth rates they achieved). Although totally efficient tax collection is an impossibility, in recent years both Shanghai and Zhejiang have achieved above-average tax income growth rates that place them among the fastest growing provinces. This shows that we cannot apply a universal rule to all provinces on the matter of the separation of tax bureaus. Of course, there are those who argue that separation and unification of tax bureaus will alternate with the passing of time. Everyone is entitled to their own opinion. I believe that the separation and unification of the two tax systems have both pros and cons; we shouldn't make hasty conclusions, as only history can reveal the truth."

In an effort to solve the problem of outdated mechanisms that already existed before the reform of the tax system, after the reform the Zhejiang Finance Bureau continued the approach of linking its operation funds to its fiscal income. The absolute tax income of each county in 1993 linked with the trade tax income was converted to the ratio of linking the tax income with the total regional fiscal income, and operation funds were, from 1994, determined by the rate as calculated in this way. The average rate across the province was 6.8 percent. On this basis, the Provincial Finance Bureau made necessary adjustments to counties with rates that were too low or too high. For example, a limit of 12 percent was set for individual counties whose rates surpassed 12 percent, and Hangzhou's rate, calculated at only 1.8 percent, was increased to 2 percent.

After the reform of the tax allocation system, fast increases in some regions' fiscal income meant that these counties had considerable amounts in their construction funds, which played a major role in upgrading their tax bureaus. The construction fund was at first withdrawn from the treasury under the category of SOE after-tax profits, but this was considered inappropriate when, in 1997, an audit was conducted by the Shanghai Resident Office of the State Auditing Administration. Later, Zhejiang province adopted the fiscal income of 1997 as the base number and changed its financial category to fiscal expenditures, at which point the operation funds of tax bureaus were properly managed and stopped increasing rapidly.

8.3. Abolishing Rural Taxations

Repeated increases in rural taxes became, over time, a fundamental principle in Chinese history. In order to alleviate social conflicts, numerous dynasties throughout history attempted to lessen the peasants' burden and consolidate their dominance by reforming the rural taxation system. Except for reforms carried out in the early Han and the Cao–Wei dynasties, these attempts rarely achieved much; all attempts to merge taxes led to a peak of heavy exactions some years later.

Since the 1980s, farmers' tax burden had been on a rise. The increase in the peasants' burden led to friction and conflict in some areas, seriously damaging relations between officialdom and the people. In order to alleviate the peasants' burden, a document issued in 1992 by the State Council entitled *Notice on Farmers' Tax Burden and Labor Management* stipulated that peasants' tax burden must be within 5 percent of average per capita net income of the previous year.

As peasants' net incomes are difficult to determine, some villages and towns exaggerated the base income in order to collect more tax, rendering the above mandated 5 percent threshold the minimum rate imposed on peasants. A *Notice on Carrying Out the Experimental Work of Rural Reform of Taxes and Fees* (No. 7 [2000] of CCPCC) was therefore jointly issued by the CCP Central Committee and the State Council on March 2, 2000. The major elements of the pilot project on rural tax reform that it pointed out were:

(i) elimination of various administrative fees, government funds or fundraising targeting the rural population such as the rural overall tax and the rural education fundraising;
(ii) elimination of the animal slaughter tax;
(iii) elimination of stipulated accumulative labor hours and compulsory labor contribution;
(iv) adjustments in policies on agricultural tax and tax on agricultural specialty products;
(v) reform of the fund application for village deductions, and establishment of the first pilot site in Anhui province.

On the basis of the pilot project, the State Council issued the document *Notice on Further Implementing the Pilot Program for the Rural Tax Reform* (No. 5 [2001] of the State Council) on March 24, 2001, stipulating that the combined agricultural tax and surcharges amount to a total tax rate no higher than 8.4 percent, of which the actual agricultural tax rate made up 7 percent, and the 20 percent surcharge, 1.4 percent. The bases of calculation of agricultural tax were to be the area of secondary contract farmland, and the average yield of five years before 1988. With the passage of time, the actual yield of China's crops had, as noted above, increased substantially since 1958 through technological advancement. But the agricultural tax nationwide was still levied according to the set-rate standard set in 1958. The average national agricultural tax rate was, as a result, extremely low relative to production. As noted by Wen Jiabao (then Vice-Premier) at a meeting on "Agricultural Tax System Reform Mobilization" held in Anhui on April 13, 2000, it was only 2.5 percent of annual production. The Anhui agricultural tax reform pilot program was, clearly, an attempt to merge taxes, placing a spotlight on the previously little-known "Huang Zongxi Law".[6]

In the past, agricultural tax reform had been a "game of interests" between grassroots governments and the peasantry, but following the issue of the Center's above-mentioned *Notice on Carrying Out the Experimental Work of Rural Reform of Taxes and Fees*, departments in charge of the agricultural tax in some provinces in central and western China joined in the game as well, even becoming winners. In order to demonstrate their acceptance of the importance of agricultural tax work, provincial-level agricultural tax departments were raised in rank to secondary bureau level; county-level agricultural tax departments were accordingly raised from group to secondary section level; and regional and city-level agricultural tax departments were raised from section to secondary division level. The reforms offered officials in these departments an excellent chance to benefit themselves. Clearly, in China, grassroots governments are unworried by changes taking place at higher levels, as benefits could be gained through these transitions; absent any transition, there would be no such chances.

As director of Zhejiang Department of Finance, I submitted a report entitled *Proposal for Tax Reform by Cutting, Eliminating and Exempting Taxes in Rural Zhejiang* to the provincial Party Committee and government in December 2001. It suggested that starting from January 1, 2002, agricultural tax and tax on agricultural specialty products should be exempted, and the rural slaughter tax and various rural fees not supported by policy should be eliminated; and starting from January 1, 2003, a tax cut of one-third should be made annually to the Five Comprehensive taxes and the Three Deductions. Supported only by individuals in the higher

---

[6] Translator's note: "Huang Zongxi Law" was so named by Qin Hui, a professor of economic history and a public intellectual at Tsinghua University. See David Kelly, "Editor's Introduction", "The Mystery of the Chinese Economy: Selected Writings of Qin Hui", *The Chinese Economy*, Vol. 38, No. 4 (September 2005).

leadership, and failing to win the support of relevant departments or the majority of officials, the proposal's future was not promising.

In order to eliminate agricultural tax, which made up less than 1 percent of the total national fiscal income while a large portion of the collected amount went towards collection costs, I successfully lobbied the support of Xie Xuezhi, Director-General of the Taxation Administration Department of the Ministry of Finance, and encouraged him to talk to the leaders in charge. The leaders said that in terms of scale of income, my proposal was reasonable. But the elimination of agricultural tax would essentially eliminate all taxation obligations between peasants and the government, as when the animal husbandry tax was eliminated in the Tibetan Autonomous Region. Opinions on taxation obligations varied widely; many were of the opinion that the agricultural tax was a nexus in the relationship between the people and the government, and this was the opinion of those opposing the tax exemption in Zhejiang.

Since this idea of the agricultural tax as a nexus relating people and government hampered the reform of Zhejiang's agricultural tax, the Department of Finance of Zhejiang province was forced to turn the proposal from "abolishing" to one of "stabilizing" the agricultural tax, adjusting (stopping) the tax on agricultural specialty products, cancelling the Five Comprehensive taxes, and cancelling the animal slaughter tax. The proposal was then handed to the State Council under the name of the provincial government. On January 12, 2002, after listening to my telephone report, Mr. Xiang Huaicheng, the Minister of Finance, expressed support for the proposal. At a National People's Congress meeting on March 5, 2002, Premier Zhu Rongji invited officials from Zhejiang to make a detailed report on the tax reform proposal to Vice-Premier Wen Jiabao. On the afternoon of March 11, I accompanied the Provincial Party Committee Secretary and the Governor to Zhongnanhai, site of the government headquarters in Beijing. After hearing the report made by Zhejiang's Party Secretary and Governor, Vice-Premier Wen Jiabao said: "There is a substantial transition of Zhejiang peasants into secondary and tertiary industries. The province is fiscally strong, which makes it a separate case from the central and western regions. It can therefore plan its own agricultural tax reform according to local circumstances." Following Wen's directives, between March 29 and April 1, 2002, officials from the General Office of the State Council Leading Group for Rural Tax Reform went to Zhejiang to carry out on-site investigations and coordination. On June 8, the General Office of the State Council issued Document No. 60 [2002], formally approving our Program for Expanding Rural Tax Reform Pilot Efforts in Zhejiang. In July of that year, rural tax reform with Zhejiang characteristics was carried out in Zhejiang, and the agricultural tax came to an end for all rice-planting peasants in Zhejiang province by 2004; it was abolished in toto in 2005.

In 2003, the Ministry of Finance and the State Taxation Bureau issued a document to incorporate the tax on agricultural specialty products into the agricultural tax, while the tax on agricultural specialty products was replaced by the lower agricultural tax. Before the opening of the Second Session of the Tenth National People's Congress, Jin Renqing, now Minister of Finance, proposed to Vice-Premier Wen Jiabao that the agricultural tax should be abolished nationally within three years from 2004. The proposal was adopted by the Vice-Premier in his Government Work Report, and in 2006, after thousands of years of history, the tax was finally abolished.

CHAPTER 9

CHINA'S REFORMS:
ARE THERE LESSONS
FOR OTHER COUNTRIES?

Arjan de Haan, Xiaobo Zhang
and Shenggen Fan

In recent years, as the economic success of China and its growing global role appeared to be sustained including throughout the 2008–2009 financial crisis, there has been a growing interest in drawing out the lessons from China for other countries. African leaders in particular have shown an interest in understanding the reasons behind its success, an interest no doubt strengthened during the African summits hosted by their Chinese counterparts. "Clearly, we all have a lot to learn from China", according to Liberian Finance Minister Antoinette Sayeh, as "China has made great progress in the past few decades in combating poverty" (*People's Daily Online*, May 16, 2007). International agencies like the World Bank, UN, and DFID have also started to promote the learning of these lessons, and indeed China's government has made it its objective to share with the world the stories and reasons for its success, as manifested in the hosting of the Global Conference on Scaling Up Poverty Reduction in Shanghai in 2004, the establishment of the International Poverty Reduction Center in China, and through the many training programs as part of its international development cooperation.

An increasing number of studies are now starting to contemplate what lessons from China may be of relevance for other countries.[1] For example, in a review chapter in the volume from the Global Conference on Scaling Up Poverty Reduction held in Shanghai in 2004, Wang (2005) summarizes the factors contributing to China's poverty reduction such as learning, decentralization, the expansion of free market, external agencies, monitoring, and the external environment that provided opportunities for collaboration and learning. Chinese cases of development projects were well-represented at the conference, with nine case studies across a range of sectors and themes. The UK Parliamentary Committee that visited China in 2008 was suitably impressed by the country's development successes, the contribution of international development and aid, and in particular the ability of China to convert relatively small-scale pilots and experiments (including those funded through international collaboration) into national programs.[2]

But what lessons are most relevant, if any? The chapters in this book have highlighted the way China has used (or was able to use) crises as an opportunity, its experimentation and regionally-specific policy formulation and reform, the sequencing of policies, information flow and consultation, and institutional capacity in addressing barriers to reforms. Which of these are of relevance to other countries, and in what way? To a certain extent, the answer to this question seems to lie in the eye of the beholder, as the following brief review of recent literature suggests.

---

[1] Earlier studies, for example in the early 1990s, focused on lessons for transition economies (Lin *et al.*, 1996), at a time when the Chinese economy was marked by busts and booms. The current wave of interest appears to have a broader focus on the developmental experience per se, often with a focus on Africa. See also the recent World Bank support for sharing experiences between China and Africa, on http://info.worldbank.org/etools/ChinaAfricaKS/resources.htm#backgroundpaper.

[2] House of Commons, International Development Committee (2009). This concluded that DFID's relationship with China provides a mutual learning experience. The Department can help transfer lessons from China's own development to other developing countries, particularly in global priority areas such as food security. It can also draw on its own innovative work in China to inform its programs elsewhere.

9.1. Views on Lessons from China

The significance of the question of lessons from China, and to some extent the controversies, is highlighted by the attention given to the question by a number of senior World Bank staff. According to Martin Ravallion (2008), a poverty specialist with long-standing experience of analyzing poverty in China (see Ravallion and Chen, 2004) and impact of development projects (see Ravallion, 2008a), two main lessons stand out from China's development experience, in particular for Africa; he also acknowledges that Africa faces many constraints that China did not face (such as political instability, inequality, demographic factors), or at least to a lesser extent.

The first lesson Ravallion (2008) highlights concerns the role of agriculture, which is in line with much of his analysis of China and elsewhere that shows how much growth in agriculture has contributed to poverty reduction. China's success in poverty reduction, in his view, illustrates the importance of promoting agriculture in the early stages of (pro-poor) growth, and supporting this through public support as well as creating market incentives. In Africa, research shows that more poverty reduction could be achieved through a stronger focus on agriculture: "African countries will have to find their own, tailor-made versions of the rural reforms and public investments that will be needed to raise the productivity of smallholders" (Ravallion, 2008).

The second main lesson from China concerns effective state institutions. As this volume has highlighted, Ravallion (2008) discusses the "importance of combining pragmatic, evidence-based policymaking with capable public institutions and a strong leadership that is committed to poverty reduction", the learning processes from local initiatives (much more difficult across African countries), and the emphasis on "searching for truth from facts". Historically, China has had much stronger and effective state institutions than African countries, "and it has no doubt helped that China did not make the mistake of believing that freer markets called for weakening those institutions". As much of the global governance literature would agree, effective state institutions are a probable pre-condition for progress in Africa, but it is equally clear that it is extremely difficult to craft them where they do not exist.[3]

David Dollar, who was country director at the World Bank's Beijing office, also directly engaged in describing what factors of China's development experience are relevant for other developing countries (Dollar, 2008). His emphasis is slightly different from Ravallion's. First, he highlights deep-seated features of Chinese culture — a Confucian ethic and its emphasis on education and very high savings rates. He adds that none of these by themselves would explain recent economic successes; for example, China's pre-1978 poor economic performance took place under the same cultural features, and indeed international experience has shown that culture by itself is unlikely to be a strong explanatory factor, and (fortunately) similar development paths can happen under different cultures.

Second, Dollar stresses the way China emphasized "Gai Ge Kai Feng", which means "change the system, open the door". This refers to the need to change the system and alter incentives and ownership, including through competition for investment between localities, thus preparing for the right investment climate, as various chapters in this volume have highlighted. It also stresses the need for opening up of the economy and welcoming direct foreign investment. Dollar is a strong believer of the role of opening up for economic growth and poverty reduction (Dollar and Kraay, 2002). But as many have stressed (e.g., Lin, 2007), it is probably the way in which China opened up and the way it was sequenced in broader reforms (as the chapters in this volume highlight), rather than opening up per se, that has been critical for its success.

Third, Dollar highlights China's investment in infrastructure as a critical lesson for other developing countries, perhaps including even India which otherwise has experienced much progress as well. The quality and benefits of infrastructure are clearly visible to any visitor to China,

---

[3] There is also an interesting potential lesson with respect to China's aid program. While China's official foreign policy principles prescribe non-interference and Chinese approaches are critical of the governance agenda of OECD countries' aid programs, China's own experience would suggest that without good governance development, investment is unlikely to be successful.

but Dollar also highlights that the infrastructure was provided through a policy of full cost recovery, with borrowing and repayments at commercial interest rates. The international community, particularly in the World Bank, has recently reaffirmed the role of infrastructure for development, partly influenced by China. In fact, China's own investment in Africa has a strong emphasis on infrastructure. But international experience has also shown that models of funding do remain problematic.

Fourth, while Ravallion highlights gains in agricultural productivity, Dollar stresses the moves out of agriculture as a key lesson. He sees migration from low-productivity rural employment to higher-productivity urban employment as an important source of growth. While the migration in China was limited due to the *hukou* system, it was sufficiently flexible to allow the movement of people that fuelled economic growth and promoted poverty reduction. The role of migration for poverty reduction in the context of a rapidly expanding and labor-intensive economy like China's is beyond dispute — indeed, empirical research shows the big impact of remittances on rural households' incomes. But it seems equally critical that China has avoided some of the worst consequences of this transition witnessed in other countries, and that the conditions under which it has managed this is unique. Indeed, Cai Fang in another context (2008) clearly stated that he is very doubtful that the lessons from China with respect to migration are of relevance to other countries.

The new World Bank Chief Economist, Justin Yifu Lin, has also described his views on the lessons from China. His earlier work (Lin *et al.*, 1996) focused on the lessons for transition countries, but his more recent work is broader in scope. In the year before being nominated as World Bank Chief Economist, when he was still director of the China Center for Economic Research at Peking University and adviser to the Chinese government, he highlighted that China and Vietnam achieved long periods of fast economic growth without implementing some conventional free-market policies,[4] whereas other countries that liberalized

---

[4] This is not necessarily inconsistent with Dollar's emphasis on China's openness, but the latter is a measure of trade flows, not a policy.

much quicker have worse records of sustaining growth and reducing poverty. As many others, Lin (2007) stresses that the gradual approach of China has worked much better (although it was also the result of the political constraint that Deng Xiaoping faced) than the shock therapy promoted and implemented in large parts of the rest of the world since the 1980s: "A gradual, piecemeal approach to reform and transition could enable the country to achieve stability and dynamic growth simultaneously and allow the country to complete its transition to a market economy." Lessons from the Chinese experience include the following: governments can take measures to improve individual incentives of state-owned enterprises; it can introduce dual-track prices and allocation systems (as discussed in this volume) to be followed by full market liberalization in due course; and it should "continually introduce the necessary regulations and laws to strengthen market institutions during the above process". However, other countries should not apply these principles or experiences in a dogmatic way. For instance, reform of the household responsibility system which succeeded in China was not successful in Russia under Gorbachev.

In a recent World Bank paper by Lin and Wang (2008), which stresses China's strategy of following comparative advantage and continuous ("market-based") learning processes, the focus is on the lessons for Africa of China's opening up, particularly in attempts to set up export zones.[5] The authors conclude from China's experience (p. 28) that liberalization itself is not sufficient to jump-start export, and that for China, system reform and opening up were equally important aspects of its development path. Export processing zones function only when the right incentive structure is in place, and an initial period of "import substitution" may be required to promote the private sector. Comparative advantage remains critical. Further, Lin and Wang note the importance of price distortions, which in their view China may have maintained for too long, and the resulting emphasis on capital-intensive industry contributed to China's

---

[5] This paper is thought to be relevant in terms of how to evaluate objectively China's experience with trade and investment integration, which may be relevant for the particular circumstances in other countries.

problems of inequality and environmental degradation.[6] Finally, Lin and Wang (2008, p. 30) conclude, as if mirroring the literature on "good-enough governance":

> "The pace of reforms, adaptation, and innovation should be commensurate with a country's development stage and regulatory capacity. China certainly did not do everything right during the trials and experimentations of the past 30 years of reforms. It paid dearly in high 'tuition'. But, as a good student, China has been learning, selectively, from the experiences of other developed and developing countries — learning well and fast. Through learning-by-doing, China is catching up at a pace that is consistent with its institutional capacity and national objectives. It is noteworthy that the pace of reforms has seldom been allowed to go beyond institutional and regulatory capacity."

This brings us to the discussion on the Washington and Beijing Consensus, a discussion that may generate more heat than light, but is nonetheless critical in the way lesson learning is and may be happening. Significantly, the term "Beijing Consensus" was coined by the former Foreign Editor of *Time* magazine, Joshua Cooper Ramo (2004). It implies distinct attitudes to development, particularly a "ruthless willingness to innovate", alongside international politics aimed at fostering international relations whilst maintaining power balance within the region. The Beijing Consensus and the development paradigm followed by China and other East Asian countries is projected as offering hope "after the collapse of the Washington Consensus". We do not believe that the projection of such opposites is particularly useful, both because the international debate has moved well beyond a Washington Consensus, and equally because the complexity of China's development makes it difficult to identify a

---

[6] Dollar (2008) also stresses the negative consequences of China's development path. As Gulati and Fan (2007) argue as well, despite successes in reducing rural poverty in China, by most estimates at least 100 million rural poor still exist. Therefore, continuing policy reforms that are based on better targeting, building institutional and human capacity as well as fostering stakeholder participation are essential in order to continue to be an international example of policy reform.

"consensus". However, it is likely that this terminology will continue to structure the way learning takes place.

This brief and selective review of the emerging literature on "lessons from China" suggests commonalities as well as differences. China's process of policy reforms supported by committed leadership and a capable administration is a common theme that comes out of all academic writings as well as more casual observations — an important lesson in itself as it demonstrates the intractable nature of problems in countries which do not have these policy conditions. But the differences that mark the broader international development debates are equally present even in this very limited sample of writings on China. For example, the role of agriculture versus other sectors; the sequencing of promotion of sectors and reforms; the process and timing of opening up; the nature of government controls, including the need for and possibility of funding of infrastructure and other public goods — all these are themes where the "lessons from China" are likely to be contested, even before we question the relevance of the experience for other countries.

9.2. The Process of Lesson Learning

Because China has adopted many policies and strategies, without counterfactuals and with successes and failure, it is hard to pin down which are the most important lessons underlying China's rapid economic growth. With the benefit of hindsight, it seems many seemingly heterodox policies can be justified as key lessons. However, it is not clear how these ideas came about in the first place.

One of the notable features in the debate so far is that there is no reference to how processes of learning happen, or ideas about how they should happen. This is partly because the agencies and people quoted in the previous section are directly involved in promoting these lessons, notably the Government of China and the World Bank. The former promotes international exchange in a broad sense, and much of the exchanges have a strong (and apparently, greatly successful) focus on "field visits" to learn from China's development experience. The World Bank promotes lesson learning through its usual channels of research and publication, uniquely now with a Chief Economist as one of its great promoters, and financially supports (as do other international agencies such as the UNDP and DFID) efforts towards "South–South learning" by government partners. The absence of reflection on the process of lesson learning is understandable in the context of the agencies that are directly engaged in this relatively new enterprise. In this section, we try to contextualize this process through a discussion of the nature of international policy transfers.

It is important to start by emphasizing the nature of learning that characterizes the policy process as described in the chapters of this volume. In China, research is seen as directly relevant to the policy process; a separation between fundamental and applied research is much harder to distinguish than in a western context. It may not be irrelevant that many of the academic researchers post-1978 had a rural background during the Cultural Revolution. Policymakers often directly engage in academic research, or in setting up think-tanks or conferences as described in the chapter by Luo Xiaopeng in this book.

The literature on policy learning and transfers shows that there is a wide range of ways in which "learning" takes place, a wide range of actors that can be involved (including government officials and civil servants, pressure groups, policy entrepreneurs and experts, transnational corporations, international and non-governmental organizations, think-tanks, and consultants), and a wide range in the political nature in which these transfers are situated (for example, the international discussions on policy convergence, liberalization, deregulation).[7] Processes of policy transfers can take manifold forms, can be voluntary as well as coercive (for example, through aid conditionality), and have been described as convergence, diffusion, learning, policy band-wagoning, emulation, harmonization, and systematically pinching ideas. One of the reasons a Beijing Consensus may gain in popularity is because its opposite, the Washington Consensus,

---

[7] The following is based on the excellent review carried out by GSDRC, commissioned by DFID China; this is available at http://www.gsdrc.org/go/display&type=Helpdesk&id=461. This uses a definition by Dolowitz and Marsh of transfers as a process in which knowledge about policies, administrative arrangements, institutions, etc., in one time and/or place, is used in the development of policies, administrative arrangements and institutions in another time and/or place.

is widely perceived to have been imposed with much economic and financial power, whereas China projects its "offer" of lesson learning in the spirit of mutual cooperation.

The process of China's domestic policy learning and transfers and the way international learning is now being promoted appear to be at different ends of the scale suggested in the literature. China's own learning can best be characterized as proactive learning and perhaps systematically pinching ideas. China continues to look at international agencies to provide international experience and techniques to address specific policy and administrative problems. Of course, these processes are not uniform — different agents have different motivations, and funding rather than ideas tends to be a critical issue at local levels. But overall, the lesson learning by China has been strongly "owned" and on an equal footing, and thus a recipe of the success that many international agencies feel their collaboration has had.

On the other hand, the process of learning that China currently promotes, for example through "South–South learning", tends to be much more supply-driven and far less systematic. The lesson learning from China tends to start from the China experience, rather than the needs of the recipient or learner. Training programs by Chinese agencies, while extremely rich in content and practice-oriented, usually do not conduct systematic training needs analysis. Neither is the audience of the lessons carefully selected, as, for example, candidates for training programs are identified by Chinese Embassies abroad (where expertise on relevant development issues may be limited).

The international literature identifies various risks of policy transfers and learning, several of which may be relevant to our discussion here (and some may have applied to China's domestic learning too). For example, policymakers may be unsure of their motivations for pursuing policy change. The "learners" may lack the understanding of the political and social contexts within which the policies operate, which may lead to uninformed attempts to adaptation of the new policy. People may also enter learning experiences with a narrow view or assumption of possibilities, and fail to look beyond the familiar. The international literature suggests that the understanding of what is being achieved by spreading policy ideas and good practice is still limited. There is great potential for lessons from

SUBJECT INDEX

AUTHOR INDEX